Awakening to the Mind of Christ

My journey into freedom

By
Linda Busuttil

Glorybound
Publishing

Glorybound Publishing
Camp Verde, Arizona
in the year 2023

Endorsements

Over the years I have been asked to write endorsements for several books. They were primarily theological in nature, pointing the church in a particular direction. Linda Busuttil in her Awakening to the Mind of Christ is theology with a face, her own. The sub-title My Journey into Freedom reveals the background for story. Her story is honest, heartbreaking and a raw account of a life redeemed by the God of grace and overflowing love. If you are broken by life's hardships, please, read this book. You will sense hope! You will know that God can restore what was lost.

If you have moved from darkness to light, then reading this book will refresh what redemption feels like. If you know people who remain trapped in a cycle of destruction, give them this book. Once you encounter divine transformation, then, then a roadmap of biblical understanding is needed for the journey ahead. Linda Busuttil does not stop with her personal story but adds a Scriptural overview of the God who delivered her.

This is pure theology, knowing God through a revelation of Scripture. Her experiences add depth to understanding Scripture. This book is a gift for everyone. It is for all of us who need God and desire to live life to its fullest, with joy and peace. I highly recommend this book. Thank you, Linda Busuttil, for sharing your life and insights for this journey we all participate in.

Dr. Stan Newton
President, Crown Institute of Theology

Joy and I have known Pastor Linda for 25 plus years. She is a powerful woman of God. Her book is life changing to those who read it. Highly recommend it.

Dr. Steve Bush
Taking Care of People International

This book is:

A triumph of God's love and mercy
A triumph of Trust and faithfulness
A triumph of Grace and Goodness
A woman's triumph against all odds
A triumph of the Overcoming perseverance of Faith.

Pastor Carl Garitson, Solid Rock Alive AZ

I have known Linda for 30+ years and I can earnestly say she has had an authentic God-encounter which has left its "mark of love" upon her life. Upon reading her book you will see her mental relocation to a much higher superior way of life found in Christ. You will be thoroughly engaged as you read and capture her awakening to the truth of her authentic God-given identity. Her perspective will set captives free from the haunting mind traffic that plagues so many people today.

You will discover who God made you to be by intentional design. Your design, purpose and destiny are not fraudulent or distorted but filled with hope and a brilliant future! As Linda points out, so perfectly, you are His Special Treasure. As she so aptly says: "Lets partner with Him by thinking like Him." These are truths she has learned, and now shares with others, to show how to practically disconnect with old destructive patterns and become renewed to what God sees in His creation called humanity.

Her clear understanding of freedom is born out of her relationship with God and Holy Spirit influence. Her desire runs clear throughout this book: Break out and be free!

Dr. Patricia Garitson,
Pastor, Solid Rock Alive

Spiritual symbol of dandelion:
Hope, resilience, strength, determination,
overcome adversity, and transformation.

Spiritual effect of dandelion:
Hope, Love, and happiness.

Literary symbolism of dandelion:
Innocence, childhood memories,
and passage of time.

Dedications

To My Parents. Courageous in light of your own stories, I deeply honor and love you both. I am grateful you were my parents.

To My Sisters Diane and Carol. You have your own overcoming victories to tell in this life. With deep respect and love for you both, we journey on together.

To My Beloved Joseph. You knew and continue to know the depths of the Revelations of Grace and more - long before I did. Oh, how I am enjoying them now! I hear you cheering me on from the "Cloud." I miss and love you. We are, forever, one.

To My Best Friend and comrade in the faith, Patricia, who laughs when I cry (only you understand), and the endless discussions of revelation that have launched us into the Life of Liberty, Himself. Forever, my friend.

To Carl, My Best Man Friend. You are a true brother, comrade, and spiritual leader. I deeply trust and love the safety of our genuine sister-brother relationship. It is an honor, joy, and at times, hilarious to live life and minister alongside you and Patricia at Solid Rock Live, Cottonwood, AZ.

To Bonnie and Cliff Mohr. My spiritual mentors and eternal friends. God brought you both into my life to answer my deepest heart cry to know Him. "No one has greater love than this- that one lays down his life for his friends. And that you both did for me. With eternal gratitude and love.

To Stan Newton, Founder and Professor of Crown Institute. The courses at the institute and your teachings gave me life-changing revelation that broke constructs of systems of belief (religion) that were barriers to a closeness with God. You told me at the point of my graduation to pray about going 'public' with the story of my journey. I prayed, and God said yes. You are the inspiration of why I wrote this book. Thank you!

To Sandra Cravens, Editor of this book. I could not have done it without you! You are a true friend and gift to me. E4 – let's do more! Time to write your own book!

To Sheri Hauser, Glorybound Publishing. Your gifted insight challenged and drew me out to go deeper helping me realize the Father's dream to have this book published and lead many to Freedom. Thank you!

Letter From Author

It has been over 30 years since my life has been radically changed. I live a fruitful and fulfilling life. I have peace, contentment, restored relationships, and meaningful friendships. The family who I love, and respect has been restored. I am a successful business woman and am still creating. I have have the answers I looked for and a deep and real relationship with God I always wanted. It goes beyond my fondest dreams. This is really real. Truly I am living the good life; liberty in Christ Jesus.

Is it still an ongoing process? Yes. I remain open to more revelation in my union with God, that matures me. Are circumstances and relationships perfect? No. But I have answers to navigate this life for an overcoming result. I do not even relate anymore to the person I was before my encounter with God and our journey together started. Has it always been this way? No. This is the reason I am writing this book.

My personal life and spiritual journey writing is for those whose heart cries want to be heard and understood. This is for those searching for the meaning of their life and wanting answers to difficult questions. To the one who wants to know God. To the one that feels trapped, as I once did, in the tormenting destructive cycles of life and want out. It is genuine hope for the despairing heart. Do you feel out of control emotionally; the words written on these pages will impart empowerment and peace to a troubled soul. Are you silently struggling? Traumatized? At the end of your rope?

I come from a place where I have experienced these emotions, mind torments, and questions, and I have been made free. With that said, I know that you can be free also. To the one that this applies to, this is why I wrote my personal agonies and victorious discovery of a meaningful life. My deepest desire is to share with you the 'light' at the end of the tunnel.

My compelling desire is that you will identify, yes, on some level with my journey and, better still, come to the realization that what God did for me He is ready, willing and able to do for you. I will present to you the choice that will enable you to discover your authentic life and purpose.

Introduction

As a result of my home environment, I grew up with a myriad of insecurities, pent-up rage, and an overpowering sense of despair and hopelessness. I was convinced I was a failure and inadequate in every aspect of my life and being. I felt powerlessness. As a result I became self-centered, controlling, and manipulating to those around me. The distorted self-image and emotions caused me alarming, destructive, and painful behavior and experiences. I lived a lifestyle of bondage.

From early childhood, I had an innate desire to know God. I was raised in a religious tradition that taught God is angry with Mankind and is a punisher for what we do wrong. This God resembled my earthly dad and mother. I concluded, who could trust a God like that? As a result, I became rebellious and revengeful out of deep rejection. I blamed Him, my parents, and for that matter, everyone, for everything that went wrong in my life.

I share intimate experiences and events of my life that defined me, told me who I was, and, at one time, I did not see any way out of the darkness I felt. Truly, for the Grace of God, there is a way out of the painful hamster wheel of destruction. My life is not like that any longer.

My greatest desire is for the reader to be able to relate your issues and personal circumstances and see your way out of them to a good conclusion and fruitful life. My journey is a spiritual one. An authentic, undeniable discovery of a relationship with God and being transformed by that union.

I went from a lifestyle of bondage ruled by a distorted self-image and emotions to a superior inner reality, our true spiritual life of peace and joy. I put into practice living from my authentic self-image and reflect that life in my earthly experience. I lay out the spiritual path of Truth in the scriptures that empower you to experience the same. My victory can be your victory. What God did for me, He has done and will do for everyone, including you. I don't always 'do it right,' but I introduce you to the ONE with the answers and the freedom you seek.

From my journey with God, I want you to know how valuable and loved you are.

Life-altering moments. I have them. You have them. Every created being has them. Throughout our lives, there are key events that happen, positive and negative, that define how we see ourselves and impact our destiny. You probably can identify many of your own. They can shape our perceptions, personalities, decisions, behaviors, and Life for better and for worse.

Unless an event interrupts these negative impressionable moments, we generally continue to live out of a false and distorted identity that formed us early on. These times are called the transformative years. We typically absorb those moments into who we are, or we change. If most of our early life experiences are positive, we can live a pretty satisfactory life. But even in the best of circumstances, one can still feel empty inside and left asking oneself, "isn't there more to this life than this?" Personally, my childhood and young adult years were not so smooth.

The following story is my journey during those transformational years; and the life-giving, spiritual discovery I had, and continue to have, that led me from a lifestyle of destruction, to Finally an Awakening of all that was preventing me from my authentic self and destiny.

My ultimate desire for authoring this book is to encourage you, those who feel trapped in a seemingly never-ending destructive cycle of any kind that you too can break free!

Chapter 1
Young and Vulnerable...

When I was in kindergarten, the school I attended was a typical Long Island, two-story brick building. It had huge, floor to ceiling windows flooding the halls and classrooms with sunlight. The stairs had cold tile floors, and the iron railings looked like looming prison bars. Someone had put a brown paper bag on my head one Halloween day as a costume. All of us children were walking down three flights of stairs. I could not see because the holes that somebody cut for me to see out of the bag did not line up with my eyes. The teacher had to pry my hands off the stair bars because I froze in fear. She took my hand and forced me to walk down the steps, still not seeing where I was going. I was terrified. I dealt with so many fears throughout my Life. I had fears of falling, heights, a fear of man, talking in front of people, claustrophobia, and many more irrational fears. Remember "show and tell" day at school, once a month? I was petrified to be in front of the class to share and talk. Every month I told my mother I was sick that day until she finally caught on.

Early in my youth, as far as I can remember, my self-esteem was quite negative. My inner dialogue mimicked the accusations, judgments, and criticisms I had routinely heard in our household. This self-deprecation eventually transformed into retaliation against my parents and other authority figures. Rejection and Rebellion were my go-to coping mechanisms, and they became comfortable companions, or so I thought. I did not talk much because I was captive to the manipulative traffic in my mind. This cognitive dissonance impaired my speaking ability; sometimes, I would stutter or not complete my sentences when I spoke. These thoughts were tormenting and frustrating, and I began exhibiting emotional fits of anger and rage. It brought periods of depression, of which I suffered for weeks. I was fearful and crushed in thought, and it prevented me from normal teenage activities. I usually did not attend school functions; if I did, I was purposefully disengaged. Sadly, I would have preferred to melt into the wall.

My school problems were numerous and dysfunctional. I was an underachiever who had difficulty concentrating, preventing me from comprehending what I was learning. I barely made passing grades and failed many. It was a miracle I graduated high school. These apparent deficits paralyzed me with heightened insecurities.

In addition to the mental and emotional torture I was experiencing in these teen years, let us now add the physical horrors of acne and braces on my teeth. My self-loathing caused me to retreat deeper into torment. My adolescent brain tried desperately to compensate for its perceived inferiority by either berating myself or building myself up. Searching for relief, I developed an imaginary friend I would talk to at night. Somehow, this aberration became a temporary answer to my troubles. As I spoke to it, I would see a cloudy form. Thankfully, this was a short-lived phase and didn't become as psychotic as it might have.

However, out of sheer frustration and anger, I elevated the level of my antics, searching for the positive affirmations I desperately needed to feel whole. I became the class clown for attention and expression. This acting out seemed to work because now everyone wanted to be my friend. I finally received the desired attention, but just like a drug, the satisfaction was short-lived and disingenuous since it was just another counterfeit for love. In response to my inner confusion and lovelessness, my poor behavior intensified. I began to have rageful fits, and by age 19, a psychiatrist declared me clinically suicidal. It seemed I had descended into the depths of hell with no return ticket. In my first marriage, I held a gun to my head, and on one occasion, I even pointed it at my husband. My emotions were out of my control, and I was desperate for relief.

To make matters worse, my psychiatrist suggested that I get a divorce from my husband and have a relationship with him. I wondered if my situation could get any worse. This deviant solution was a case of a mental health professional manipulating a vulnerable young woman into deeper sickness. Somehow, even in my sick mind, this perverted suggestion frightened me. I could not trust anyone, and I felt hopelessly trapped. There were no answers. I dove deeper into looking for ways to escape from being severely depressed, and I became a very paranoid person.

Violent thoughts against myself and others, I would self-inflict pain by digging my fingers into my arm and causing myself to bleed. All the while feeling self-hatred, guilt, and shame. In this unrelenting and miserable state, hopeless, I naturally turned to alcohol and drugs for welcome relief. I could numb my emotions and escape into a fantasy world of Life. This lifestyle and tormenting cycle would last until I was 39 years old.

Chapter 2
My First Encounter With God...

I always wanted to know and experience God. As a young girl, at the age of 9, I was walking home from elementary school. I would love to pause and eat the prolific honeysuckle vines that covered the bridge over the parkway on the way home. As I watched the cars speed underneath the overpass, I would imagine jumping from that bridge to end the tormenting thoughts.

One day I was eating that honeysuckle, and the tangible Presence of God engulfed me with His brilliant light and right beside me. He was real, and I could see Him. I did not know that I was seeing, by the eyes of my spirit, into the spirit realm back then. I was immediately filled with feelings of love, joy, and peace that I had never experienced before. Little did I know that this brief encounter with His brilliance, followed by this sensation of completeness and wholeness, would become a reference point for the rest of my life in seeking Truth. It placed a seed (Love) in my heart that yearned for more. It created a journey and destination point I would insatiably seek to reproduce. This experience began my first life-altering event.

During this miraculous moment, I spoke to Him (God). I told Him that I always wanted to know Him. I was happy for the first time I could remember and never wanted it to end.

The joy and completeness I felt caused me to skip all the way home. Sadly, that encounter and the feelings I experienced were short-lived. The moment I entered my house, the dysfunctional and toxic environment, I fell into a cycle of emotional turmoil again.

I continued a long destructive path dotted with alarming and desperate emotional outbreaks. I would go on binges of not eating for weeks to see how long I could go. Once, after being intoxicated and up all night, I fell and cut my chin open. I had to go to an emergency room, reeking of the smell of alcohol. The doctor asked me if I needed help with my drinking. I became indignant and told him that I didn't have a problem. I suffered from constant anxiety attacks and spent much time seeking medical help. Treatment was barely helpful as attendants would have me breathe into brown paper bags or put my head in buckets of ice water. I desperately screamed at God to help me while blaming Him and others for why I was the way I was.

I was raised in a traditional church and belief system. As a young girl, I even knew within myself that Jesus Christ was God. Having that knowledge, I could not translate it to mean anything to me personally. I practiced a traditional religion with no relationship with God and no personal benefit. I recall making a distinct negative decision because of what I was taught, "Oh, what's the difference what I do. I'm a sinner. God is angry with me; not happy with me; I'll probably go to hell, so I might as well have 'fun' and do what I want to do." It was a defining moment that spiraled me down the path I chose. It was a turning point, for the worse, in my life. I made a willful, rejected, and angry decision, not knowing who God really was.

Chapter 3
My Second Spiritual Encounter ...

I had another encounter with the Lord at 33 years old. I went to a birthday party and as a gift, I "generously" bought a bottle of wine for a close friend. I fully expected him to open and share its contents with me. In essence, I bought it for myself, and I was pretty annoyed when he did not share it with me. After all, it was after breakfast. I left in a huff to buy my own bottle but remembered that it was Sunday, and the liquor stores were closed for a few more hours. Remember when businesses were entirely closed on Sundays?

As I walked down that Florida street, at 2 pm, on a sunny afternoon, I was suddenly surrounded by an even more brilliant light than the sun. I stopped walking and was compelled to look at the light that encircled me and my heart was ignited within me. I was being talked to. In a nanosecond, I had an epiphany about the consequences of my downward spiraling Life. I experienced feelings of hope stir inside me (remember that seed that was planted?).

I had personally encountered God's tangible Presence again. The void I desperately sought to fill was complete again! His manifested Presence (light) instantly freed me from craving alcohol and drugs. I bypassed the liquor store and returned to my car. This event interrupted my lifestyle of the "not-so-rich and famous," and it was a turning point in the right direction. I was "hit by the sun (Son) of His love". That same day, I called a friend who had been sharing with me how he stayed free from alcohol and drugs. I began embracing Anonymous meetings. I went to those meetings for six years. During those years, I dealt with emotions that sent me into panic attacks and "close encounters of the 3rd kind"! I was what they called "stark raving sober." Oy vey. It was not fun, but it was truly better than the alternative. But truly, for the grace of God.

I was free from alcohol and drugs, but my panic and torment continued. I joined every anonymous self-help group known to man. I pursued psychological counseling, and I delved heavily into the metaphysical realm. Eventually, I wandered into the occult. I dabbled with psychics, seances, cultic conferences, practices, meditations, medicine, and even conjured up spirits. I was seeking God, ignorant that it was through an inferior counterfeit realm. No wonder my outcome was also dark and inauthentic to the superior realm of Truth.

I believed that I was progressing in enlightenment and getting closer to God. I spent thousands of dollars that I couldn't afford, looking for answers and relief, to no avail. I had an insatiable desire for the supernatural and to know God and experience that peace, love, and joy I encountered when I was 9. I went deeper into my spiritual quest but was always unfulfilled. I was as empty and desperate as when I started. There was a massive vacancy in my soul that was never filled or satiated. An inner cry of desperation occupied every moment of my Life.

Now, in Arizona (long story), I knew I was going nowhere fast after years of self-help groups, counseling, and searching. I was still empty, with no peace and no God connection. It was time to get honest with myself. One afternoon, I was in my small condo, closed the blinds, and started yelling out for God. I recalled, later on, this happened at the same time of day, 2 pm, as my previous encounter with God that delivered me from alcohol and drugs. I demanded of Him, to show Himself to me and answer my questions. After all, I said, if you are Love, why is there such pain and evil in the world? By the Spirit, I heard Him say, "I gave man free will."

For the first time in my life, I understood I blamed Him for everything. Now His answer, reality, Himself, will set people free of wrongly accusing and assassinating God's character. It was in my distorted self-image that I did not take responsibility for myself, not knowing who I really was. It was everyone else's fault. A fair statement would be, we just don't know what to do to change anything, including ourselves. Avoiding truth (and Truth) was my usual reaction. I would have liked to have told you that God's answer satisfied me, but it didn't. My answer was, "Well, anyway…" as I shot another question to Him. Even as I reflected, I had an uncanny sense of peace, hearing Him calmly answer my demanding questions. My ignorance was glaring, but my heart was sincere. I had to know God!

God Answered my Heart's Cry…

In the months following the second encounter with God, He "sent" me a wonderful woman who had a personal connection with Jesus. I was ignorant of this ability to have an intimate relationship with the Creator of the Universe. He was always, "out there." I, at the time, was a hairdresser by vocation, and the connection was divine because she had been praying for God to show her a place and a person to have her hair done. It was heavenly, indeed, but not a natural fit. I was into the occult, and she was into Jesus. As we talked, I distinctly remember thinking, 'oh, great, I have a bible banger in my chair.' She and her husband were preaching the gospel worldwide, so it took a while for us to connect deeper. I must admit, her speaking of "signs and wonders" piqued my interest in the supernatural.

By her third visit, she shared the "good news" of the gospel of the Kingdom of God, but it was almost meaningless to me at the time. She asked me if I knew who Jesus was. I said yes, He is the Son of God, but still, it meant little to me. She said, so effortlessly, "if you believe in your heart and acknowledge with your mouth who He is, you can have a relationship with Him." Her assuredness was compelling. She clearly enjoyed that peace and joy that I was looking for. She put her hands on me to pray for me, and the power and presence of God were so intense I backed up against the wall. His tangible manifestation was pure bliss, and my heart immediately resonated with His Presence.

So it was that I was born again, awakened anew, in 1988, at the age of 39. I believe that I am not alone in my search to connect with God. All of humanity desires to know His love and find their purpose. Only a loving Father would put that innate desire in the hearts of Mankind and has an answer for each one of us. Even the wisest man on earth (Solomon) tells us this:

Ecc 3:11

> *"He has made everything beautiful in its time. He also has planted eternity in men's hearts and minds [a divinely implanted sense of a purpose working through the ages which nothing under the sun but God alone can satisfy], yet so that men cannot find out what God has done from the beginning to the end."*

Man's heart longs to experience what he senses instinctively; his eternal God-given identity and a relationship with His Heavenly Father.

Relationship with Loving Father God...

How does a person strike up a relationship with the Creator of the Universe? Most people think choosing a relationship with God was their original idea. I was shocked when I found that God first chose to have a relationship with me. It actually pleased Him. What a welcome revelation! I didn't have to perform to "get to Him."

Ephesians 1:4-5

> *"Even as [in His love] He chose us [actually picked us out for Himself as His own] in Christ before the foundation of the world, that we should be holy (consecrated and set apart for Him) and blameless in His sight, even above reproach, before Him in love. For He foreordained us (destined us, planned in love for us) to be adopted (revealed) as His own children through Jesus Christ, in accordance with the purpose of His will [[b]because it pleased Him and was His kind intent]"*

He reveals to us we are His beloved children.

Eph 2:4-8

> *"But God—so rich is He in His mercy! Because of and in order to satisfy the great and wonderful and intense love with which He loved us, Even when we were dead (slain) by [our own] shortcomings and trespasses, He made us alive together in fellowship and in union with Christ; [He gave us the very Life of Christ Himself, the same new Life with which He quickened Him, for] it is by grace (His favor and mercy which you did not deserve) that you are saved (delivered from judgment and made partakers of Christ's salvation).*

And He raised us up together with Him and made us sit down together [giving us joint seating with Him] in the heavenly sphere [by virtue of our being] in Christ Jesus (the Messiah, the Anointed One) through [your] faith. And this [salvation] is not of yourselves [of your own doing, it came not through your own striving], but it is the gift of God;."

The gospel is so simple and it is good news. It is about our loving relationship with God. It bypasses the intellectual mind and all the strivings of performance of a religious system. It is a free gift; you are and always were unconditionally loved; come as you are. Because the world's standards condition us to always have to work to get, we might find it difficult to believe that He chose us first and all we have to do is receive from Him.

The offer of Salvation, the fullness of the Life of God, is not a reward or result of our good or bad behavior. He rescued us back to Himself because He loves us and did what we could not do for ourselves.

John 3:3

"Jesus answered him, "I assure you and most solemnly say to you, unless a person is born again [reborn from above— spiritually transformed, renewed, sanctified], he cannot [ever] see and experience the kingdom of God."

Because I acknowledged and accepted who He is; Savior of Mankind; I instantly became aware and an heir to the Kingdom of God.

We truly see, by His Spirit, the reality of our origin and our purpose comes into focus. We can see and know Him relationally. Wow! Once I tasted this realm, I realized I wanted all God had for me. And there was more!

Chapter 4
The Baptism of The Holy Spirit

After I acknowledged who Jesus is and accepted Him, I went a step further. It was three months later, on May 16, 1988. This wonderful woman and her friend who knew God asked me, "Do you want the Baptism of the Holy Spirit and to speak in a spirit language?"

I hadn't a clue what that meant, but I heard myself say, "I want all that God has for me. What is this baptism that Jesus imparts?"

Matt 3:11

> *"I indeed baptize you with water because you changed your minds for the better, heartily amending your ways, with abhorrence of your past sins. But He Who is coming after me is mightier than I, whose sandals I am not worthy or fit to take off or carry; He will baptize you with the Holy Spirit and with fire."*

This baptism first happened on the day of Pentecost in the "Upper Room" when Jesus reappeared to His disciples 50 days after His resurrection.

Acts 2:4

> *And they were all diffused throughout their souls with the Holy Spirit. They began to speak in other (different, foreign) languages (tongues), as the Spirit kept giving them clear and loud expressions [in each tongue in appropriate words].*

This baptism was an example of God, the Father, who lives in us all, and is in us all.

(Eph.1:23) He connects our hearts as One.

I asked Jesus, by faith, to baptize me in the Holy Spirit. This "Baptism" immediately connected my heart and mind as one, with Him, within me. Supernaturally, I began to speak in my spirit language. I did not know or study this language. As I released the Holy Spirit to speak from my heart, God gloriously replaced the "empty hole in my soul" with His love and genuine *knowledge of Him*. This "knowing" is the revelation of Jesus Christ and not an "intellectual" knowing in my head but a "spiritual" knowing in my heart. It is an intimate experience with Father God. Finally, I had achieved that "peace that passes all understanding" I had only heard of before this time. My mind found out what my heart knew. I had contact with God. Miracles abound, and I have never been the same since. I tell the Lord; eternity is not long enough to express my gratitude and love!

Now, I had the knowledge of God by the Holy Spirit. He opened the eyes of my heart to see the spirit realm of the Kingdom of God. I leaped off my couch, and spontaneous praise and thanksgiving came out of my mouth in my spirit language. I have quite a fondness for the Holy Spirit. I am head over heels in love with Him. He is the One and the only One that truly enlightened me with a revelation of Himself, God.

The Holy Spirit gives us the power to live the Kingdom life here on earth. We need our relationship with God to be relevant to this Life we live here on earth. Otherwise, it is just a form of godliness without tangible evidence of Truth. This enabling is where the rubber meets the road. This empowerment is the Holy Spirit's expertise! All the victory

Jesus obtained for us; the Holy Spirit enables us to live the overcoming Life on earth as it is in heaven.

Acts 1:8

> *"But you shall receive power (ability, efficiency, and might) when the Holy Spirit has come upon you, and you shall be My witnesses in Jerusalem and all Judea and Samaria and to the ends (the very bounds) of the earth."*

The Holy Spirit is the connection to the supernatural dimension of the Kingdom of God…

The Holy Spirit instantly delivered me of some unpleasant and tormenting things I did in my Life. I had a foul mouth that immediately stopped. My need for promiscuous behavior ended as it was an attempt to fill my emptiness with a relationship. I became modest in my behavior and dress. I went through my closet and gave away every 'thread' of clothing that spoke of a promiscuous lifestyle.

This act was incredibly freeing as the tormenting thoughts and pictures left.

A supernatural Peace flooded my mind. Once I opened my heart and acknowledged what He provided for me, I slept like a newborn baby. Tears of gratitude and joy replaced my torment. I met the Prince of Peace, Himself, Jesus. There are challenges to that Peace, but I am quicker at choosing not to tolerate the interruption. Many nights I would dialogue with the Lord and thank Him for providing me a sweet and secure sleep. Now that's the conversation I love to have going on in my head! He is so faithful and the true rescuer.

Prov 3:24

> *"When you lie down, you shall not be afraid; yes, you shall lie down, and your sleep shall be sweet."*

John 14:27

> *"Peace I leave with you; My [own] peace I now give and bequeath to you. Not as the world gives do I give to you. Do not let your hearts be troubled, neither let them be afraid. [Stop allowing yourselves to be agitated and disturbed; do not permit yourselves to be fearful and intimidated and cowardly and unsettled.]"*

You are His child and are secure in Him as you sleep. Sweet dreams...

I continued to allow the Holy Spirit to connect me to the supernatural Life of His Spirit.

I began learning to identify God's voice, discovering the remarkable Life of the spirit, and practicing applying this knowledge in this journey called Life.

The Holy Spirit truly is our companion in every way and in every day. It is a rewarding and worthwhile walk with Him.

Gal 5:25

> *"If we live by the [Holy] Spirit, we must also walk by the Spirit [with personal integrity, godly character, and moral courage—our conduct empowered by the Holy Spirit]."*

I take my lead from the Holy Spirit in my daily conduct. I have learned that we have been given dominion authority in this Life over everything. We are the victors, the overcomers, and Holy Spirit always leads us into triumph. Living with this mindset creates success. Paul reminds us:

II Cor 2:14

> *"But thanks be to God, Who in Christ always leads us in triumph [as trophies of Christ's victory]..."*

Things may not always be perfect, right, or easy, but He always works all things for our good when we persevere. We are IN HIM! In victory!

I Cor 6:17

> *"But the one who is united and joined to the Lord is one spirit with Him. "*

Being joined to the Lord is not only excellent but also causes me to become aware, in a good way, of my independent ways. I was disconnected because I trusted no one and knew no other way. It was a survival tactic for me. Choosing to unite and surrender my stubborn ways to His loving will was an excellent choice! It is a process and always to my benefit. We realize His motive is always love, and He is all-knowing and wise.

Isa 55:8-9

> *"For truly, my ways are not His ways, and my thoughts are not His thoughts."*

I have come to the conclusion; it is illogical not to do things as He advises and leads us to. He is God!

Let's settle this: Jesis is God...

Where does God start with a person like me? Looking back, it felt like I must have given Him that "deer in the headlights" look when I realized the Creator of the Universe was trying to connect with ME! God knew what I needed, and He started my journey precisely where I needed Him to start: at the beginning.

That's where we should start on our journey together – at the beginning. I will get right to the point. Jesus is God, and He was God in the flesh. And He is God currently in our flesh!

John 1:1-4

> *"In the beginning [before all time] was the Word (Christ), and the Word was with God, and the Word was God Himself. He was present originally with God. All things were made and came into existence through Him, and without Him, was not even one thing made that has come into being. In Him was Life, and the Life was the Light of men."*

The **Mirror Bible** comments on that verse: "Suddenly the invisible, eternal Word incarnates (becomes visible in the form of flesh and blood) as in a mirror and is now confirmed in us!" (I will be using this translation a lot in this book as I feel its revelation and translation is most illuminating)

This act is the most accurate tangible display of God's eternal thought, and it finds expression in human Life! The Word became a human being; we are His address; He resides in us! He captivates our gaze! The glory we see is not a religious replica; He is the authentic begotten son. The glory (that we lost in Adam) returns in fullness! Only grace can communicate truth in such a full context!

What did this mean to me? What does this mean to you? First and foremost, it satisfies the deepest longing in our hearts. To know God and to be known by Him. answers the fundamental question in every person's heart, 'who am I?' 'Why am I here?' Secondly, it assures us that we are never alone. I had the most challenging time being by myself. The emptiness in my heart was so painful and loud. I would spend days away from my apartment with friends just so I wouldn't have to be alone. I was in the habit of filling my every moment with people, relationships with men, strangers, alcohol, and drugs so that I was not by myself.

Once I met the Lord, I stopped doing the things that would be an artificial substitute for fulfillment. I chose to open up to God and be honest which resulted in becoming genuinely satisfied and complete. I distinctly remember a time I was agonizing over my sense of loneliness. Crying on my couch, I told God what I was feeling. He appeared to me and listened intently with such compassion and said to me, "I understand." I was flooded with the loving person that He is, satisfied that He understood and related to me. It is so kind and comforting to be listened to and understood. But He did not leave me that way. He filled me with a sense of completeness and the depression, self-pity, and deep despair left. Only He can do that if we allow Him.

Heb 4:15

> *"For we do not have a High Priest who is unable to sympathize and understand our weaknesses and temptations, but One who has been tempted [knowing exactly how it feels to be human] in every respect as we are, yet without [committing any] sin."*

Not only does He understand us, but we can trust Him, also. Why, can we trust Him, you and I ask? Because He is also the Truth!

What is the Truth? ...

What is Truth? Truth is the person, Jesus. We say that "Jesus is a relationship, not a religion." He is not a system or a formula to perform by. He is not a bunch of rules or man-made ordinances to live your Life by. Our relationship is based on love and trust because He is the Truth, and our Life.

John 14:6

> *"Jesus said to him, I am the Way and the Truth and the Life; no one comes to the Father except by (through) Me."*

To see Jesus is to see the Father - One and the same. It is a relief to know Him, The Truth, that does not change according to man's whim. We can look at Jesus and into His Life and know Father God.

John 14:9

> *Jesus replied, have I been with all of you for so long a time, and do you not recognize and know Me yet, Philip? Anyone who has seen Me has seen the Father. How can you say then, show us the Father?*

It is also a game changer. When we know the Truth, then we can spot the lie. Lies about God, ourselves, and our situations; anywhere deception tries to creep in; we can go to the Truth and be set free. That's a far cry from being tossed to and fro with every wind of doctrine. Jesus, the Truth, silences all the voices of doubt, unbelief, and confusion. We know who to go to. We mature and become secure.

Eph 4:14

> *"So then, we may no longer be children, tossed to and fro between chance gusts of teaching and wavering with every changing wind of doctrine, [the prey of] the cunning and cleverness of unscrupulous men, in every shifting form of trickery in inventing errors to mislead."*

Even well-meaning religious denominations can and are misleading. Why? Because they are performance-based and man-created doctrines. It leaves us always striving to attain God's approval while teaching that we cannot have what God has promised until we go to heaven. This erroneous view is called "futurism," which believes that the Kingdom of God is distant and not yet. (Delay) This teaching is not Truth. The Truth is Jesus, and He has already accomplished all He set out to do to establish His Kingdom. As He said on the cross, "It is finished."

John 1:4-5

> *"In Him was Life [and the power to bestow Life], and the Life was the Light of men. The Light shines on in the darkness, and the darkness did not understand it or overpower it or appropriate it or absorb it."*

Jesus is God, the Way, the Truth, and the Life. Whether we believe Him doesn't change the reality that He is the Truth. The only difference is the people that do not accept Him, the Truth, won't experience Him. He is to be experienced, and nothing can overpower Him. His light will illuminate the darkness, and we will see the truth and be set free. The grace and kindness of God will make anyone tender to Him. Feel free to share this experience!

One day, I was talking with Him about the particular healing I desired. I saw it in the Word but was struggling to believe it for myself. I said, to Him, 'I am having a hard time believing that. Would you please help me?' He said, 'I can work with that.' He appreciated my honesty, as if He didn't know, and helped me to receive my healing.

John 8:36

> *"Who the Son sets free is free indeed..."*

The Truth is; He has already set us free. When you and I accept what He has obtained for us, on the Cross, through His finished work, that is when we receive our freedom.

Chapter 5
A Quality Decision; Choosing to Change

We should always be willing to truly consider evidence that contradicts our beliefs and admit the possibility that we may be wrong. I heard and agreed with this appropriate quote: "Intelligence isn't knowing everything; it's the ability to challenge everything you know." Goodness, this can be challenging! Indeed, when it came to the knowledge of God, I was misinformed and immature.

When I was first presented with the evidence of the Word of God, I had the choice to believe this new information or not. This decision was (and "still" is) the most important one I have ever made about anything. This one decision has literally transformed and continues to change me and my Life. I emphasize the word "still" because the point of this entire section is that this choice is a continual option.

I allowed the Truth, the Word of God, to take first place in my life, and this action has served me well. I believe He is the highest form of Truth, and I follow His guidance regardless of my emotions. This trust was a massive shift for me as it countered everything, I thought I was sure of - yet my Life was a mess. Everything in my Life at the time contradicted what God was saying, who I was and what was mine. Focusing on my relationship with Jesus and receiving revelation from the Scriptures continues to reveal the Truth of who He is, who we are, and the victory He has obtained for us. What did it take for me to arrive at this destiny?

In the first five years of my relationship with the Lord, I turned the TV off and did not read other books or materials that were not the Word or had anything to do with the Word of God. I began the process of renewing my thinking to the Mind of Christ. The Word of God says that we have received the Mind of Christ when we accept Him. I still had tormenting thoughts in my mind for a while, but I persevered, choosing to believe this new Truth. I reasoned with myself, "what else is there to do and what do I have to lose?"

I tested and practiced the Truth like this; whenever I felt rejected, paranoid, and had negative thoughts, I would remind myself what God said. I would speak it out loud. Sometimes, exposing the lies that came to my mind required input from other people I trusted. Their answer was always different than what I was thinking. This is how I learned about the enemy's deception - how clever and cunning he was to instill fear and get me to question my identity and authority.

However, with my newfound Truth, I envisioned him running away with his tail between his legs! I enjoyed that sight immensely, and then I would thank God for my victory!

Of course, there was still a steep learning curve. On many occasions, I quietly exited the Church during the fellowship, hoping no one would see me. After all, I would think, "they'd probably rather talk about me than to me." This insecure and self-absorbed behavior was obviously in great need of healing. With help from my mentor, I learned to challenge these thoughts by confronting them head-on. If no one was talking to me, then I would purposefully go and talk to them. This new paradigm required some boldness, for sure. I remember having these mental arguments going on inside, and

I would make myself reenter the building through the back door, hoping no one noticed I had left. It all seems so crazy when I look back at that battle. I learned to engage with people confidently, and it was so fulfilling! Good things happen when one is God-centered rather than self-centered.

I found, over and over, that the thoughts and belief systems I struggled with most of my Life were not of God. It was out of a false identity, believing lies about myself and not knowing God. I learned to replace those thoughts with the Truth of what He said about me and my situations by meditating on His thoughts - and my behavior changed accordingly. What a miracle in my Life!

I also learned that I do not have to remain the same, and neither do you! In Truth, we all have become someone new through what Jesus did for us. What does all this mean? Let's begin with what Jesus has done for us. (2 translations of Paul's understanding)

II Cor 5:17 (Amp)

"Therefore, if anyone is in Christ [that is, grafted in, joined to Him by faith in Him as Savior], he is a new creature [reborn and renewed by the Holy Spirit]; the old things [the previous moral and spiritual condition] have passed away. Behold, new things have come [because spiritual awakening brings a new life]."

II Cor 5:17 (Mirror)

"Now, in the light of your co-inclusion in his death and resurrection, whoever you thought you were before, in Christ you are a brand-new person! The old ways of seeing yourself and everyone else are over.

Acquaint yourself with the new!

This understanding began the change in me and will in

you too. Choosing to meditate and believe what God said about me in His Word continued a great awakening in my spirit to Truth. I began to acquaint myself with the "new me" and meditated on that. I started to really like the "new me" and become comfortable in my own skin.

Faith in God started to ignite in my spirit. My perspective began to orientate to the spirit realm rather than the natural realm. When we do this, with the help of the Holy Spirit, we begin to spiritually awaken to the actual reality of who we are in Christ and the newness of Life that He has for us.

There is no One and nowhere else to go for Truth and Life. He is the first Word and the last Word on everything. We get to know our Heavenly Father and ourselves by what He thinks and says through our relationship with Him and His Word.

God's Thoughts and Ways...

His thoughts and ways were absolutely not my thoughts and ways. EVERYTHING I thought and believed was different from Him.

Isa 55:8,9

> *"For My thoughts are not your thoughts, neither are your ways My ways, says the Lord. For as the heavens are higher than the earth, so are My ways higher than your ways and My thoughts than your thoughts."*

It is an astounding awakening to discover God's thoughts and get to know Him for who He really is. Contrary to all my preconceived ideas, the introduction to think another way, His way, was and is a welcomed relief. At the same time, it challenged my natural habitual thought life and belief patterns.

The Mind of the Flesh and the Mind of the Spirit...

Why are our natural thoughts (without God) so off course?

Rom 8:7

> *"[That is] because the mind of the flesh [with its carnal thoughts and purposes] is hostile to God, for it does not submit itself to God's Law; indeed, it cannot."*

So, we come to the revelation that this natural realm's thinking patterns were dictated by the physical senses and became a prison to us. These thoughts are in opposition to all that God says. This natural sense knowledge, at one time, defined God, us, and our lives. I learned, and I trust, the scriptures, along with my testimony, will awaken this to you. Living this Life, dictated by the sense realm is the opposite of the Truth of God.

Once, God said to me...." You have mind idolatry" Every natural thought influenced by my physical senses came against the knowledge of God. My way of thinking exalted itself as Truth. Thought patterns were my idols, including myself. I also learned that I was proud and arrogant in believing what I thought was the truth. I thought I knew it all and relied on myself in all circumstances. When meditating on God's thoughts and ways, I could see that my thoughts (without God) were inferior, dark, and a lie against who He is and whom He made me to be. Talk about being your own worst enemy!

I had a belief system of erroneous philosophy and religious tradition, and I did not trust others or God. It was about me, me, and me. The Holy Spirit showed me this type of thinking was idolatry, and to be free, these thoughts must be brought into the obedience of Christ by renewing my mind. I needed a foundation built on the Truth. I was willing to change and learned that God was delighted to teach me. We will gain understanding and revelation of the Truth with a teachable heart. The following verse should be very encouraging.

Mark 4:25

"For [a]whoever has [a teachable heart], to him more [understanding] will be given; and whoever does not have [a yearning for truth], even what he has will be taken away from him."

The Spirit of Truth, Himself teaches us. Jesus has already provided freedom from the fallen mindset.

Rom 8:9

"But you are not ruled by a flesh-consciousness (law of works), but by a spirit-consciousness (faith); God's Spirit is at home in you. Anyone who does not see themselves fully clothed and identified in the Spirit of Christ, cannot be themselves." (Mirror)

Jesus awakens us to our freedom to live our authentic self, Spirit beings having an earthly experience and He has cleansed our flesh-consciousness.

Heb 9:14

"how much more will the blood of Christ, who through the eternal [Holy] Spirit willingly offered Himself unblemished [that is, without moral or spiritual imperfection as a sacrifice] to God, cleanse your conscience from dead works and lifeless observances to serve the ever-living God?"

We are born of the Spirit of God, and His Spirit renews our thinking. We are thereby transformed. It is an inside job.

John 3:6-8

> *"That which is born of the flesh is flesh [the physical is merely physical], and that which is born of the Spirit is spirit. Do not be surprised that I have told you, 'You must be born again [reborn from above—spiritually transformed, renewed, sanctified].'"*

The key to being ourselves is to be conscious of Spirit. We do this by faith. Thinking God's thoughts will enlighten us about who we already are in Him. Looking at Jesus, we identify with Him and see ourselves. We look into the law of liberty, the Word of God. It is the law of Life itself, Our Life. We see and are set free to be our true authentic selves, made in the image and likeness of God. This is the wonderful discovery of who we are in Christ.

James 1:25

> *"But he who looks carefully into the perfect law, the law of liberty, and faithfully abides by it, not having become a [careless] listener who forgets but [h]an active doer [who obeys], he will be blessed and favored by God in what he does [in his life of obedience]."*

We are free from the darkened understanding by the law of liberty. We begin to see our true selves and Life in Him. This revelation is good news!

I would make it a practice to identify contrary thoughts by the Word of God. When a thought felt uncomfortable, I would examine the source of that thought.

Knowing that only goodness and light come from God, any counterfeit was easily exposed. The turmoil caused by the lies quickly left, and I would promptly experience His peace. The peace that passes all understanding.

Isa 26:3

"You will keep in perfect and constant peace the one whose mind is steadfast [that is, committed and focused on You—in both inclination and character], because he trusts and takes refuge in You [with hope and confident expectation]."

Phil 4:7

"And the peace of God [that peace which reassures the heart, that peace] which transcends all understanding, [that peace which] stands guard over your hearts and your minds in Christ Jesus [is yours]."

The peace we long for is assured by being in our right minds, the Mind of Christ. This space is our rightful place. Everything fights for our focus - distractions, and lies of all kinds. Just adjust your focus and put it on Him; there it is, peace. This peace is not temporary or fleeting but is an inner serenity that only being in Him brings.

The peace that is already in us will resonate with God within us.

John 14:27

"Peace I leave with you; My [perfect] peace I give to you; not as the world gives do I give to you. Do not let your heart be troubled, nor let it be afraid. [Let My perfect peace calm you in every circumstance and give you courage and strength for every challenge.]"

Jesus gave us His peace. This is our genuine reality. Every day, moment by moment, we can adjust our focus on our inner peace, which is Him.

The Battle has been Won...

It was a spiritual battle that was won. No longer do we have to feel powerless, overwhelmed, and defeated. The truth is Jesus won the victory and gave us the authority and power to enforce it. We now live an abundant and overcoming life. Let's face it - Some challenging situations will arise, but we are well-equipped to handle them.

Luke 10:19

> *"Listen carefully: I have given you authority [that you now possess] to tread on [a]serpents and scorpions, and [the ability to exercise authority] over all the power of the enemy (Satan); and nothing will [in any way] harm you."*

Luke 10:19 (Mirror)

> *"See, I have given you authority to trample upon serpents and scorpions and every powerful symbolic disguise of the enemy. Nothing shall by any means nullify your authentic identity! Your likeness is secured in me!"*

So, you see that we are not helpless victims anymore!

I like what the Mirror Translation says in this scripture:

II Cor: 4-5

> *"Every lofty idea and argument positioned against God's knowledge of us, is cast down and exposed to be a mere invention of our own imagination. We arrest every thought at spear point – anything that could possibly trigger an opposing threat to our redeemed identity and innocence is taken captive.*
>
> *The caliber of our weapon is empowered by the revelation of the ultimate consequence of the obedience of Christ."*

This Truth encourages me to live fearlessly. Let it encourage you also! With this in mind, we can choose to have an overcoming attitude in our daily Life.

Chapter 6
Our Fight is Not With People...

I struggled with this concept for quite some time. I was convinced people were my problem. I went around the same mountain of challenges over and over again. I thought: " if it weren't for them, I wouldn't have these problems, and I wouldn't be this way." Did I mention I was argumentative? I always 'explained' how I was right and they were wrong.

Before my transformation, I was continually fed up and discouraged by people. I was learning new ways to see old problems and knew there was an answer to this dilemma. I became willing to challenge what I believed – again – a key to accepting positive change. What was Jesus telling me in His Word? What light could He shed on this problem area for me? The revelation was life-changing.

I began to understand that my struggle was not with flesh and blood but with my own darkened understanding and deceiving spirits. The battlefield was in the mind.

Eph 6:12 (Mirror)

"People are not the enemy, to target one another is to engage in the wrong combat. We represent the authority of the victory of Christ in the spiritual realm. We are positioned there; we confront the mind games and structures of darkness, religious thought patterns, governing and conditioning human behavior."

For as long as I can remember, my relationship with my earthly Dad was volatile and unhealthy, to say the least. I said it was white, and He said it was black. Both of us, being rebellious and angry, came to many verbal and physical blows that ended up outside on the front lawn for all the neighbors to see. My mother just stood by and watched. I did not understand why she did not intervene. It was a sign of betrayal to me. Screaming at each other every night at the dinner table was routine. I can still hear the sound of his fist going through the basement door and his deep cry of frustration and anger.

I am grateful it wasn't me that night. I used to hold my breath as I heard him walk down the hallway, drunk, passing my closed bedroom door. I prayed he would not open the door to pick a fight, only to punish me in the end. I remember being punished for about 9 months for having poor grades. I sat on the back porch day after day, not allowed to see any of my friends until he finally relented his harsh discipline. Needless to say, my grades did not get any better. Exasperation was a continuous experience for me. I left the house as soon as I was able.

I have a powerful example the Holy Spirit showed me about the weapons of our warfare are not physical but divinely powerful to destroy the structures of darkness that can become strongholds!

Years later, as my mind was being renewed by the Spirit, this happened...

I was talking with my dad and mother at the time, and my dad had become argumentative with me, as usual. My mother, listening to the conversation, kept saying, "your daughter is agreeing with you." I would repeat what I was saying to my dad, and he got more and more angry. I got quiet, looked inward to the Holy Spirit, and silently asked Him to help me. He opened up my spiritual eyes and showed me that every time I said something to my dad, the words I spoke went in his ears twisted. I literally watched, by the Spirit, the words approach his ears and then twist. He had a filter that caused him not to hear what I was saying correctly. The Holy Spirit had me pause, then softly and slowly repeat what I was saying differently. He finally heard that I was agreeing with what he was saying and the whole situation de-escalated. This life-changing moment gave me deep insight into what I have been dealing with since childhood.

The good news is that even if others do not change, we can be the solution and have a better outcome when we have an understanding of the underlying spiritual problem. The enemy loses control, and God has the influence of His divine nature in us.

Think of this; would we continue to look through a distorted window or eyeglasses if we could just simply clean the glass or change prescription lenses?

I know this firsthand. Many a stronghold in my thinking has been taken down with an awareness of this physical vs. spiritual issue. I have learned to ask questions or repeat what I am hearing when I feel 'triggered' or threatened. This clarity exposes any threat or misunderstanding that I may be entertaining and will diffuse the situation. My hearing has become sensitive to the Holy Spirit so He can catch my attention, so I am not reactionary but responsive in love. This is freedom!

Like the distorted lenses, that's the way rejection, rebellion, hurt, etc. works to cause problems in our lives. These emotions are the filters that we look, feel and see through. These painful or defective areas in our lives act as lenses that distort our seeing people and circumstances clearly, clouding our perception. As a result, improper strongholds are created and control our lives until they are broken. The Word of God is what is going to bring these strongholds down!

I am so grateful to the Holy Spirit. I listen to him in most of my conversations. When I don't is when I could be reactionary, and the conversation with anyone can go 'squirrely' at any time. Most people, including myself, can look and listen with a distorted filter until the Holy Spirit deals with that stronghold. However, if we choose to see with the law of liberty, the Word of God, that stronghold will be dealt a final blow.

Amazing things happened as I was learning and becoming more willing to see myself and others the way Jesus sees and does. He changed my stubborn heart - that vowed never to forgive - into a heart full of compassion and forgiveness. I also became responsible for my choices. It didn't stop there. He healed my heart, so I yielded to the Holy Spirit to break other strongholds in my Life. All the masks, filters, and facades I had put up started to be dismantled, one by one and sometimes instantly as revelation illuminated my heart. The love of God will continue to change every heart and do for us what we cannot do in our own strength.

Phil 2:13

> *"For it is [not your strength, but it is] God who is effectively at work in you, both to will and to work [that is, strengthening, energizing, and creating in you the longing and the ability to fulfill your purpose] for His good pleasure."*

As you might have guessed, I had another hurdle in my Life I needed help and healing for. I had deep wounds in my heart concerning my mother. I always felt I did not measure up, and I could never please her. I was keenly aware of her distance from me as a young child. Her constant criticism and 'scolding' were a source of rejection and depression. I did not know what to call it then, but today, I would call it disdain. Disdain is defined as "unworthy of one's consideration or respect" or "with contempt." This feeling defined me, my self-perception and I reacted with self-hatred. I was constantly asked, "why can't you be like your sisters?" To me, she was downright mean. I remember once in junior high school, my birthday was the next day, and my mother would not let me set my hair because I was being punished for something. I felt so ashamed of my hair and painfully self-conscious of my looks. I was insecure and self-conscious, to begin with, and this hatefulness destroyed any trust I had in my mother. In my eyes, she was my enemy. I was a target for her anger, and I felt I had to watch my back. Our relationship got worse.

I was shattered when my mother told me she didn't like me. As I got older, I gave her good reason not to like me. She would continue to remind me of my past mistakes (even from 50 years previous) despite the radical transformation in my Life due to the Lord. She made it a habit of asking my sisters questions about me, what I did or said, not asking me directly, while I was standing right there in the same room. One of my sisters once said to her, "well, why don't you ask her… she's right here?" It was cruel and rude, to me, to be treated that way. Even when my father almost died (ruptured appendix), my mother withheld that even though we had spoken on the phone while he was in the hospital. I learned many things were withheld from me from just conversation with my sisters.

This seeming "disdain" for me never changed – even until the day she passed into heaven. There was no warm hug, no hopeful words of forgiveness, nor acknowledgement of any positive feedback. I was the one who initiated the "I love you." Sadly, I was without a mother as a friend for her lifetime. In spite of her feelings towards me, God beautifully restored the distorted perceptions I had about her (and my father) by giving me a new set of lenses.

With healing, I learned from my Heavenly Father that He was my all and all. All the nurturing, acceptance, and love I desperately needed came from Him. He began to teach me, by our union and the Word of God, He was the One to fill, satisfy and make me whole. He told me to stop going to people who could not and weren't meant to meet my needs. This instruction did not come easy for me since I so desperately wanted the approval of my parents and others. I allowed Him to work in my heart to stop placing false expectations on others and making them responsible for my fulfillment. He alone is the One that fills the emptiness in our souls and completes us.

Psa 68:5-6

"A father to the fatherless, a defender of widows, is God in his holy dwelling. God sets the lonely in families, he leads out the prisoners with singing;

Psa 16:5-11 (paraphrased)

You, Lord, are all I have, and you give me all I need; my future is in your hands. How wonderful are your gifts to me; how good they are!

I was so bankrupt in my soul. He began to fill my severe lack, and as a result, my behavior began to change. He gave me mentors and friends (like family) who understood and went through similar things as I did.

As I matured in the Lord, I realized and acknowledged the

brokenness in my parents' lives. They had their hurts and struggles. The more I received my needs met by the Lord, the more I grew in understanding and compassion for them. I became more interested in who they were and all they had endured. They had deep hurts and experiences that impacted their lives. They were doing all they knew how to do to live Life. I realized my choices hurt them, and I was genuinely sorry. I went to both of my parents and asked them to forgive me without expecting anything back. My dad said, 'yes, I forgive you.' My mother gave an angry stare and withheld a response. It would have been nice, but it did not matter. What mattered was I felt genuine love for them and repentance for what I had done to hurt them.

Through God's healing, my respect and appreciation for my parents were restored. I love them and can see all the wonderful things they imparted into my Life. I see the gift of God in each one of them, and I am profoundly grateful they were my parents. A month before my mother passed, I wrote a letter to her and told her all the wonderful things I admired and loved about her. I told her some things I had learned and how I was grateful she was my mother.

She replied, "That was a sweet letter."

I was free whether I got a reply or not.

With my sisters, I had the honor and opportunity to pray some of the Psalms for my mother the evening before she passed and joined my dad in heaven. The next morning, I watched as the Lord opened her spirit eyes, her face lit up with expectancy as she saw the family that awaited her on the other side, and then she immediately left. I heard, by the Holy Spirit, the welcoming cheers from family and saw her dance towards her loving Heavenly Father. My heart is filled with joy that she now experiences the love of Father and that she is completely free.

I had the privilege and joy to see, by the Holy Spirit, both of my parents enter heaven. My dear husband as well. That would take another book to share, but I would like to share more about the vision of my mother's passage. I heard cheering at first in the Spirit; then I saw confetti-like substance all around her falling through the atmosphere of heaven as she twirled and danced into our Glorious Heavenly Father's embrace. My mother and father loved dancing. My sisters and I enjoy it also! You couldn't get my parents off the dance floor. They outlasted many of us on the dance floor and they were well into their 80s! Father God said to me "your mother had the first dance with me and the second dance with your dad." This was so heartwarming and loving for Him to share with me. Made me happy to hear.

In my opinion, my mother was one of the most physically beautiful women I knew. After a battle with cancer, I saw, in the Spirit, that God restored her to her youthful beauty. This vision was so comforting to me.

She had a heart of deep compassion for all she met and a deep concern for all Mankind. She had such wisdom and some profound questions to which she now has the answers. She was so funny, in a very Yiddish way. I am grateful for my Jewish heritage that I have from her side of the family.

My dad asked me to forgive him one year before He left this earth. I was grateful we had a mutual healing before he left to continue his destiny.

I know today that they both love me.

My joy is in knowing that my parents are in the cloud of witnesses, along with my precious Beloved husband, Joseph, who entered heaven way too soon for me. He was the kindest man to me. He was a good friend and the funniest man I have known. He loved God and was a gift to me. Now, they are cheering me on. We are on the same team and complete our lives together as one.

Heb 11:40

> *"Because God had us in mind and had something better and greater in view for us, so that they [these heroes and heroines of faith] should not come to perfection apart from us [before we could join them]."*

Heb 12:1

> *"Therefore then, since we are surrounded by so great a cloud of witnesses [who have borne testimony to the Truth], let us strip off and throw aside every encumbrance (unnecessary weight) and that sin which so readily (deftly and cleverly) clings to and entangles us, and let us run with patient endurance and steady and active persistence the appointed course of the race that is set before us."*

This truth about the cloud of witnesses is so comforting and our current reality in Christ. We are all one, never separated in His love. The ones on the *other side* are championing us!

For you that have had people leave this visible realm, let your heart be encouraged. We are not separated. They are living out their destiny and participating in our lives; God is fulfilling their purpose and ours together. We are one body; we are family.

Rom 8:37-39

> *"Yet in all these things we are more than conquerors and gain an overwhelming victory through Him who loved us [so much that He died for us]. For I am convinced [and continue to be convinced—beyond any doubt] that neither death, nor Life, nor angels, nor principalities, nor things present and threatening, nor things to come, nor powers, nor height, nor depth, nor any other created thing, will be able to separate us from the [unlimited] love of God, which is in Christ Jesus our Lord."*

God's love not only changed my heart but has filled me with overflowing love, peace, and hope. The process of choosing what He says about me is more rewarding and addicting than the pain of the contradiction of lies that the enemy of my soul speaks. I honestly can be my own worst enemy. It has taken longer than I would like to admit, but forgiving and being kind and loving to myself is a liberating experience. Only Jesus awakens us to our authentic self and our oneness in Him. I do not strive to be, but I just am.

Chapter 7
The Enemy and His Plan

John 10:10

> *"The thief comes only in order to steal and kill and destroy. I came that they may have and enjoy Life, and have it in abundance [to the full, till it overflows]."*

The thief comes to steal, kill and destroy. The darkened understanding, of who we are in Christ, is a thief. It distorts, perverts, and corrupts who we are and steals our destiny. Jesus, the good Shepherd, came to rescue us, reveal our authentic identity, and give us back our abundant Life in Him. We know who wins.

The great deception of the enemy is for us to doubt God and who we are. Early on, one tactic is to deceive us by questioning our very own identity and bring confusion about who we are. Next comes the rejection of self and God. If the enemy can pervert our thinking, he can distort and counterfeit God's intended goodness for our lives. He is out to rob our destinies and make a mockery of God. Well, enemy, your charade is up! The lies have been exposed. You've been undone!

I John 3:8 (Mirror)

> *"Sin's source is a fallen mindset from the beginning! For this purpose the Son of God was revealed! His mission was to undo the works of the Devil! To discover one's authentic sonship in God, is to discover true freedom from sin. We are*

born of him and his seed remains in us; this is the only possible reference to sober up the mind from the intoxicating influence of deception."

For many of my young years, I was plagued with the thought of my identity, who am I and what is my purpose? Everyone on the planet naturally has asked this question, right? Simple answer: our authentic identity is in God. We are born of Him; out of His love. We are the beloved children of God. We are chosen of God to be exactly who we are in our mother's womb for His loving purpose.

Jer 1:1

"Before I formed you in the womb I knew [and] approved of you [as My chosen instrument], and before you were born I separated and set you apart, consecrating you; [and] I appointed you as a prophet to the nations."

You and I are not a mistake. We are not an "oops" in our conception, in our gender, or our destiny - no matter what circumstance brought us here. We are wanted, loved, and born from God's desire for us from and for eternity.

Let this sink deep into your heart; read this over and over…This is the Truth about you. You are God's child. All other thoughts try to intoxicate you with deception. Don't buy the lies.

You are made in His image and likeness. You are just like your Heavenly Father. Smile.

Gen 1:27

"So God created man in His own image, in the image and likeness of God He created him; male and female He created them."

He is the One that wanted you.

John 1:13

> "...who were born, not of blood [natural conception], nor of the will of the flesh [physical impulse], nor of the will of man [that of a natural father], but of God [that is, a divine and supernatural birth—they are born of God—spiritually transformed, renewed, sanctified]."

Eph 1:5

> "For He foreordained us (destined us, planned in love for us) to be adopted (revealed) as His own children, sons and daughters, through Jesus Christ, in accordance with the purpose of His will [[a]because it pleased Him and was His kind intent]—"

His purpose for us...

Rom 8:29-30

> "For those whom He foreknew [of whom He was [a]aware and [b]loved beforehand], He also destined from the beginning [foreordaining them] to be molded into the image of His Son [and share inwardly His likeness], that He might become the firstborn among many brethren."

Eph 2:10

> "For we are God's [own] handiwork (His workmanship), [d]recreated in Christ Jesus, [born anew] that we may do those good works which God predestined (planned beforehand) for us [taking paths which He prepared ahead of time], that we should walk in them [living the good life which He prearranged and made ready for us to live]."

Let's live the excellent Life that He has made ready for us to live. Let's not let a defeated enemy steal from us!

II Cor 5:17

> *"Now, in the light of your co-inclusion in his death and resurrection, whoever you thought you were before, in Christ you are a brand-new person! The old ways of seeing yourself and everyone else are over. Acquaint yourself with the new!"*

When we discover Christ, in us, from God's point of view, we discover ourselves and every other human life from God's point of view. In other words, we no longer know Christ and others from a human and religious point of view.

Jesus reveals the Truth about us, not just potentiality. We needn't "strive" to become. The Truth is, "I am" - not "I am trying to be." He reveals our true identity: the enemy came to kill, steal and destroy by deceiving us into a distorted image of ourselves and corrupting God's original design and plan for our lives. Game over!!

Jesus Defeated our enemy...

Relax; the battle has been won.

Col 2:15

> *"[God] disarmed the principalities and powers that were ranged against us and made a bold display and public example of them, in triumphing over them in Him and in it [the cross]."*

GOD undoes the evil works of the enemy, disempowers the enemy, and frees our minds from the intoxicating influence of deception!

Every evil work of the enemy, every lie, every corrupt thing, every torment against you and I, Jesus disempowered, destroyed, defeated, and gave us victory.

You might be asking yourself what I asked myself at

this point: "You mean to tell me I have been deceived and deluded about myself and others this whole time?" Numerous people get angry when they realize they were wrongly taught or wrongly believed for whatever reason. I was angry at the lies but then immediately relieved and grateful to find out what the problem was and how to get me fixed! I have always been an individual who looks for a solution. Now, I know it is Jesus.

These scriptures of Truth rocked my world right side up! I finally understood who the enemy was. Deception, a distorted image of myself. The torment of guilt, condemnation and shame, all broken by the triumph of the Cross. The dominance of the tree of the knowledge of good and evil, hard work and labor, ended.

Religion is stripped of its authority to manipulate me with guilt. The law of works, including all principalities, all authority, every dynamic influence, any governing system that tries to rank above and over us on the basis of performance and wants to define us has been destroyed. Nothing has dominion or power over us. Everything by the only ONE POWER, HIM, has been brought under the dominion of grace where the Christ-life rules. Holy Spirit is our best friend. Not only did He reveal to me the enemy and all his lies but He shows me (and you) the way to walk out my freedom by revealing the Truth about who I am and who God is in me.

Jesus made us Free, and I wanted to Live Free!...

I Cor 15:57

> *"but thanks be to God, who gives us the victory [as conquerors] through our Lord Jesus Christ."*

My friend, He has given you and me the overcoming victory!

John 8:36

> *"So if the Son liberates you [makes you free men], then you are really and unquestionably free."*

Col 2:8 (Mirror)

> *"Make sure that you become no one's victim through EMP-TY philosophical intellectualism and meaningless speculations, molded in traditions and repetitions to mankind's cosmic codes and superstitions and not consistent with Christ."*

We are not a captive and not a victim. Jesus breaks all yokes of bondage to deception! Jesus made us free!

Another scripture speaks to this. Always learning but never coming to the knowledge of the truth. I was experiencing an endless, painful cycle of searching through other philosophies and modalities of healing and not coming to the Truth.

II Tim 3:7 Amp

> *"[These weak women will listen to anybody who will teach them]; they are forever inquiring and getting information but are never able to arrive at a recognition and knowledge of the Truth."*

The web of deception prevents us from arriving at the knowledge of the Truth. The example of the hamster going around and around on the wheel is appro pro. In other words, the continual pursuit of knowledge that parades itself as truth, is the hamster wheel—the cycle of always attaining more understanding and not experiencing true freedom.

All self-help systems of belief about higher realities, how to get to God and have personal change, proved worthless. It leaves one going in endless circles of defeat. I have been in all 12-step programs and read most self-help books known to man. Although they are offered with good intentions, elements of truth and some positive suggestions, one can be deceived into thinking that if I talk about my problems long enough, this is the path to freedom. True freedom remained aloof. It turned out to be an endless cycle of reliving the nightmares and fueled self-justification. It confirmed why I felt what I felt but was never able to create solutions. All it did was perpetuate self-pity and enforce the idea that no one else understood me except the *club*.

I became an island to myself and those who thought like me. It brought isolation from the Body of Christ and worsened my distorted image. I was being taught that I had a disease that could not be cured rather than that I was made perfect in Him. The steps of the program stated that God could be anything you desired Him to be according to your understanding – (a very generic, nondescript entity). That allowed us to create an image and likeness of who we thought Him to be.

That sounds good until you realize we came up with a God of our understanding out of our distorted perceptions and pain without knowing who He truly is. I might add, here, we already had a distorted image of Him. I am grateful I got to the honest place where I said, "Well, I really don't know God, nor understand Him, or like Him."

I demanded to know who He was and that He explain Himself. That was my heart's cry out of being a self-righteous individual.

Oh, the lure of systems, programs, and formulas that keep a person striving to get to God and to be someone we already are. It keeps us striving to get to where we have arrived through Jesus. It is twisted thinking, defying the Truth itself!

Truth is, God is the One who created us, reaches to us, loves us, understands us, believes in us, accepts us, has set us free from all sin (distorted image) sickness and disease and has a hope and future for us, being in union with Him. End of program.

The one main thing that all self-help improvement programs miss is - the ONE main thing! The self-improvement programs exploit our ignorance about our TRUE origin and our redeemed innocence. I have scripture for this.

II Cor 4:4 (Mirror)

> *"The survival and self-improvement programs of the religious systems of this world veil the minds of the unbelievers; exploiting their ignorance about their true origin and their redeemed innocence, The veil of unbelief obstructs a person's view and keeps them from seeing what the light of the gospel so clearly reveals; the glory of God is the image and likeness of our Maker redeemed in human form; this is what the gospel of Christ is all about."*

I attended self-help meetings while getting the Word of Truth in my spirit for about a year. Finally, in one session I was attending, the light went on! I got a revelation (Holy Spirit) that what was being identified by the leaders of this meeting as a "disease" was, in reality, "sin." And, as result, the revelation was that I had been forgiven and freed from the wages of this sin, (distorted image) which causes death. Death, in the sense of living way out of my true design. The Truth is, even if it was a disease, Jesus bore all our sicknesses and diseases! Jesus freed me to make choices: to be led by Him or controlled by the flesh's (sense realm) cravings. I never went back or looked back.

Yes, I get counsel from time to time from spiritual friends or advisors to talk things out or pray with those walking the talk, but all my deep help comes from the Lord. All revelation and healing are centered around what Jesus did to give me freedom and remind me who I am in Christ. He never leaves us the same but always continues to enlighten us to see our true selves in Him. Such love!

Rom 5:8

> *"But God shows and clearly proves His [own] love for us by the fact that while we were still sinners, Christ (the Messiah, the Anointed One) died for us."*

It is true freedom to get off the hamster wheel of religion, philosophies, and traditions of men. It is the Truth that breaks us out of the cycle.

II Tim 3:5

> *"...holding to a form of [outward] godliness (religion), although they have denied its power [for their conduct nullifies their claim of faith]. Avoid such people and keep far away from them."*

I see "religion" as a belief system that can replace, deny, and minimize the Truth and power of God. It can create distance from our loving Father by replacement leaders and often negates what He has already accomplished for us by creating performance goals. It is an outward display of Godliness, without inward change.

I know. I tried. I was a fraud on the inside and tried to cover it up with what I said and did. I could not change anything in and of myself. Looked good on the outside but struggled within. All the right rhetoric and still empty inside. Sound familiar?

The Lord spoke to me and says to you, also, "Beloved, I am the true vine, you are the branches. Know you abide in me. You do nothing without me. All things are possible in me, with me. In me, I have set you up for success."

An independent lifestyle is superficial and futile. Wisdom of God is not the wisdom of this world…

Jam 3:14-17

> *"But if you have bitter jealousy and selfish ambition in your hearts, do not be arrogant, and [as a result] be in defiance of the truth. This [superficial] wisdom is not that which comes down from above, but is earthly (secular), natural (unspiritual), even demonic. For where jealousy and selfish ambition exist, there is disorder [unrest, rebellion] and every evil thing and morally degrading practice. But the wisdom from above is first pure [morally and spiritually undefiled], then peace-loving [courteous, considerate], gentle, reasonable [and willing to listen], full of compassion and good fruits. It is unwavering, without [self-righteous] hypocrisy [and self-serving guile]."*

Here comes another amazing part of the journey. It takes courage, personally, to surrender to the lead of the Holy Spirit and to question and let go of belief systems and thought processes that are contrary to what Jesus says and thinks. After all, what is left? Nothing. At first, I felt empty and fearful of letting go of what was familiar and all I had been taught. As I submitted my mind to God's thoughts, He revealed my false teachings and opinions. I had defined myself by a twisted image of myself and God. I was guilt-ridden and working my way to God for His approval.

Why do we cling so tightly to our old ways of doing and thinking when they are clearly not working for us? Why do we shy away from this change when we are offered a personal, loving relationship with the Creator and a life of promise? The hesitancy is rooted in our fear and unbelief. Perhaps our strong sense of self will be lost? Maybe we won't get our needs met? No control? This is the superficial, "earthly wisdom" spoken of in the scriptures. Trust issues seem to surface when change is required. The opposite is actually the Truth. It is the lies and distortions that are controlling us! When we awaken to our authentic identity, who we are in Christ, and see Him for who He really is, we come into our full dominion and authority. We are led and we lead by love because we have His nature. The Truth is - we drop the inferior life and gain all that Christ has given us in our co-resurrection with Him. This life IS the Superior Reality. We have Wisdom from God, the spiritually moral and spiritually undefiled us. I'd say this is a good trade!

Phi 3:8-9

> *"Yes, furthermore, I count everything as loss compared to the possession of the priceless privilege (the overwhelming preciousness, the surpassing worth, and supreme advantage) of knowing Christ Jesus my Lord and of progressively becoming more deeply and intimately acquainted with Him [of perceiving and recognizing and understanding Him more fully and clearly]. For His sake I have lost everything and consider it all to be mere rubbish (refuse, dregs), in order that I may win (gain) Christ (the Anointed One). And that I may [actually] be found and known as in Him, not having any [self-achieved] righteousness that can be called my own, based on my obedience to the Law's demands (ritualistic uprightness and supposed right standing with God thus acquired), but possessing that [genuine righteousness] which comes through faith in Christ (the Anointed One), the [truly] right standing with God, which comes from God by [saving] faith."*

What did I think I had that was worth holding on to in light of knowing Him? As I have shared with you so far, my life was a mess. I had continually harbored negative feelings of inferiority, depression, anger, self-rejection, confusion, lack, fear, paranoia, the need to perform to please, torment, unfulfillment, and on and on. The liar makes us believe that we are giving up everything to follow Jesus and that we will miss out on something – especially control. The lie is that we will lose control. The truth is, without God, we are being controlled by every distortion the enemy can throw at us. When the lens is cleaned, we see that we are replacing an old and deluded inferior life for a new and promising superior life. It is a no-brainer.

Jer 29:11

> *"For I know the thoughts and plans that I have for you, says the Lord, thoughts and plans for welfare and peace and not for evil, to give you hope in your final outcome."*

He has given us a future and a hope. It's the abundant good life Christ has given us.

Chapter 8

Consider God's Love...

When we consider Him, we begin to recognize that we are His Beloved Children, born in His love, by His will. We embrace our origin and purpose. We shake loose the grips of performance and truly accept God, our Beloved Father.

I John 3:1 (Mirror)

> *Consider the amazing love the Father lavished upon us; this is our defining moment: we began in the agape of God-the engineer of the universe is our Father! So, it's no wonder that the performance-based systems of this world just cannot see this! Because they do not recognize their origin in God, they feel indifferent towards anyone who does!"*

Recognize, Beloved of God, you are His Child, born in His love, by His will.

I thought I was crazy!... I sometimes, literally, could not connect the dots. I experienced what it was like to be schizophrenic. The definition of schizophrenia: a mental disorder; a breakdown in the relation between thought, emotion, and behavior, leading to faulty perception, inappropriate actions and feelings, withdrawal from reality and personal relationships into fantasy and delusion, and a sense of mental fragmentation. If we are honest, we can all identify with these issues to different degrees. It's the only thing the enemy of our soul, deception, has against us.

The Spirit of God can dismantle any delusion, disorder, false perceptions, fantasy, and fragmentation of the mind. Jesus performed this miracle several times in the New Testament. However, we are counseled to participate in this healing by "renewing our minds." I have had my greatest deliverance from bondage by the revelation I have received by renewing my mind according to the Word of God.

Eph 4:23 (Amp)

> "and be continually renewed in the spirit of your mind [having a fresh, untarnished mental and spiritual attitude]..."

Eph 4:23 (Mirror)

> "Be renewed in your innermost mind. (Ponder the truth about you, as it is displayed in Christ; begin with the fact of your co-seatedness.) This will cause you to be completely re-programmed in the way you think about yourself!"

And furthermore:

Vs.24

> "Immerse yourself into this God-shaped new person from above! You are created in the image and likeness of God. This is what righteousness and true holiness are all about."

This transformation happens in the spirit of your mind, awakened by truth on a much deeper level than mere intellectual or academic consent. As you read and believe what the scriptures say, you will discover that you are who God says you are. Then the living waters from your innermost being will flow.

It is our mind that has been veiled by darkness; we were darkened in our understanding! Our thoughts were reduced to the soul realm reference, knowing ourselves and one another merely after the flesh. Nothing is wrong with our design or redemption; we were thinking wrong! For our thoughts to be rescued from the dominion of darkness, Jesus, as the incarnate image and likeness of God, has gone into our darkest hellish nightmare, faced our cruelest judgment and fears, and died our death!

This is the mystery that has been hidden for generations since Christ died. We were co-crucified and raised with Christ! This fact brings absolute closure to every reference we have had of ourselves as a result of Adam's fall! And while we were dead in our sins and trespasses, God co-quickened, co-raised, and co-seated us in Christ!

Now, we all with unveiled faces may behold the glory of the Lord as in a mirror! And be radically transformed in our thinking to rediscover his image and likeness fully redeemed in us!

Let us rediscover that we are the sons and daughters of God! The Word allows us to shed the lies of darkness; thus, we live in the light of our full identity in Christ. The behavioral side of life will take care of itself. We will naturally and progressively begin to line up with who we are. This is a true awakening to the mind of Christ!

This is a true awakening to the mind of Christ!

This new life is superior. It is a far cry from struggling to perform. We have already "arrived." We ARE the new creation in Christ Jesus - NOW. Religion and traditions of man are guilty of putting everything, including our hope, into a future rather than our present reality.

The Grace of God

God rescued us. He set us free. He reached into the depths of our despair and futility and did for us what we were not capable of doing for ourselves. This is boundless love. Let us now become awakened to the freedom we have in Christ!

Eph 2:5-6

> *"This is how grace rescued us: while we were yet in that state of deadness and indifference in our deviations, we were co-quickened together with Christ! We had nothing to do with it. Grace freed us, once and for all from the lies that we believed about ourselves under the performance driven system, and now defines our authentic identity! We are co-included in his resurrection. We are also co-elevated in his ascension to be equally present in the throne room of the heavenly realm, where we are co-seated with him in his executive authority. We are fully represented in Christ Jesus."*

Francois DuToit (author of the Mirror Translation Bible) says this: "We have wasted so much time trying to get there, when "there' is where we are to begin with! Our joint position in Christ defines us; this can never again be a distant goal to reach through religious devotion or striving; but it is our immediate location."

This is a key concept in my entire purpose for writing this book. It is time we choose to break free from old thinking, put on our 'Mind of Christ," and dive into a new Truth and awaken!

John 1:17

> *"For the Law was given through Moses, but grace [the unearned, undeserved favor of God] and truth came through Jesus Christ."*

Moses represents the system of laws and performance (religion) as the basis for one's standing before God. Jesus

Christ came to set the captives free. Moses represents the Old Covenant. Jesus represents the New Covenant. There was a significant shift in our standing before God at the cross. We are no longer to be judged as sinners but as righteous. We now represent Jesus as in a mirror on this earth. He is the essence of grace and Truth! We are born of Him. He is the life of our design on display – the Firstborn. We are to imitate His way.

Grace prevails against the system of performance. Jesus Christ is incarnate grace and truth! And we are in Him. He is the life of our design on display in human form, as in a mirror. Grace and Truth are our states of being in Him. He is our completeness. This is the real deal! Thank you, God!

His hand of grace has been extended to us. Will we accept?

We are just like Him in this world...

Another critical scripture that emphasizes our identity in Christ:

I John 4:17

> *"So now, with us awakening to our full inclusion in this love union, everything is perfect! Its completeness is not compromised in contradiction. Our confident conversation echoes this fellowship even in the face of crisis; because as he is, so are we in this world-our lives are mirrored in him."*

Did you know that Jesus considers us blameless as He is blameless? His perfect love has been deposited in us, so we may have confidence that when we face the enemy of scrutiny, we are considered pure as snow. How many times has religion, institutions, leaders, teachers, pastors, or clergy emphasized this Truth to you? I am willing to bet that few you know have uttered these words. Sadly, this "gold" in scripture has been glossed over and minimized for eons.

Bear with me for a minute because this next concept may be hard to receive. We are in this world, but we belong to another Kingdom. Our authentic self and superior reality are in the Kingdom of God. As it is in heaven, so it is in this world for us. This scripture clarifies:

1 John 4-5 (Amp)

> *"They [who teach twisted doctrine] are of the world and belong to it; therefore, they speak from the [viewpoint of the] world [with its immoral freedom and baseless theories—demanding compliance with their opinions and ridiculing the values of the upright], and the [gullible one of the] world listens closely and pays attention to them."*

Perhaps this sounds intangible, but it is the Truth and the basis of our faith. (If you are wondering why I always capitalize the word Truth – it is because Truth is the person of Jesus). His Grace accomplished for us what we could not do for ourselves. This Truth is eternal and a current reality. This Truth is the basis for my transformation from a life of contradictions to one of hope and fulfillment.

From our restored union with Jesus, we discover that our True origin is in God - beyond our natural conception! This origin is not about our biological lineage or whether we were a wanted or an unwanted -child. This is about our God-begotten heritage. We are his dream come true and not the invention of our parents. You are indeed the most incredible idea God ever had.

Chapter 9

Walking by Faith in The Grace of God...

As I continued to renew my mind, I faced many contradictions in my behavior to who God said I was. I made new choices with His help.

As I continued to renew my mind, I faced many contradictions in my behavior to who God said I was. I made new choices with His help.

I had little integrity before my transformation. I would say one thing and do the opposite. I would make plans and commit to doing something with someone but change my mind sporadically. I was pretty selfish, unreliable, and untrustworthy. God (Holy Spirit) convicted me about this behavior. He told me I was lying. I answered, "Who, me?"

He said, "Let my yes be yes, and my no be no."

Mathew 5:37

> *Let your Yes be simply Yes, and your No be simply No; anything more than that comes from the evil one.*

I learned to rely on God's best decisions before committing to anything and followed through. If something legitimately interfered with my intention, He led me to ask for forgiveness and release me from my commitment. I learned accountability and responsibility [which is Kingdom behavior], and it freed me from the bondage of guilt. It matured me and helped me be wise about who, what, and where to invest myself and my time. I am now known for my word; it is good, and I can be trusted.

I had another similar character flaw that needed remedy. I was late for everything- all the time. The Lord told me I was being disrespectful and stealing people's time. I immediately repented and stopped doing that. His guidance has been so helpful in freeing me from such flaws. My life is much more orderly, and I am, most of the time, early. If I am running late, I always call the person and apologize. These issues may sound simple, but they all negatively impacted my life. My relationship with God transformed my thinking, and my behavior effortlessly changed and positively impacted my relationships. All thanks to Holy Spirit.

Why is repentance necessary? Remember that repentance means changing one's mind, which naturally translates into changed actions.

Prov 23:7

> *"For as he thinks in his heart, so is he [in behavior—one who manipulates].*

We will know ourselves and others by what we do and say. If we think like God, we will act like God. In this manner, we exemplify God's outrageous loving will and transform lives on earth – as it is in Heaven!

Out of control emotions…

What I thought about myself was truly evident in my be-havior. As a young person, my emotional life ruled me. It was all I knew, and I had no way out. I was destructive towards myself and others. I would control people and my circumstances through outbursts of anger and exasperation.

Fear was a way of life. I lacked self-discipline. My natural senses ruled me, period.

Mixed in with all those negative emotions, I also had positive ones. Thank God, because little did I know that these were my gifts that would later need cultivating. I have always been a compassionate and passionate person. Whether concerned about people, animals, or this earth, I cared deeply and naturally. But I couldn't bear fruit from my giving because I didn't have a handle on the source of my God-given talents at that time. I wanted to solve all their problems for them. In other words, I wanted to be their "God." My intentions were good, but my foundation was unstable.

I would spend hours and days with people listening to their problems, trying to counsel and improve them. I was playing the role of Savior to them all. In a way, I think I was trying to heal myself. Later as I renewed my mind and received healing, I realized these gifts of passion and compassion would be used greatly in the Kingdom of God.

To my despair, my emotions manipulated me. It was a way of life for me. My fits of anger turned to rage and ended many a relationship and marriage. I lived with the guilt and condemnation from the fruit of that behavior.

The Word of God revealed that I lived in a distorted fantasy and reacted out of that illusion. None of it was real or what God had in mind for me. I wasn't able to separate my emotions from reality. I hurt people and picked hurt people to have a relationship with. The result was always the same - a vicious cycle of feeling isolated, frustrated, guilt-ridden, depressed, bitter, and pitiful.

I have shared some of my behavior during this time, but not all. I belabor the point because I hope you can appreciate the severity of the transformation. If I could be healed, anyone can be healed. I was so exasperated and explosive that I would beat my fists on walls, scream, and break windows and valuable things I cherished. I was grateful I did not physically injure or kill myself or another human being. I would recklessly drive my little sports car 120 miles an hour on the interstate highway while intoxicated. Then there's the silent treatment. I did not talk, answer or acknowledge someone if I felt they had done me wrong. That rage turned inward; I became depressed and filled with self-loathing.

The depression kept me from going anywhere for weeks. I was so angry I would just about starve myself. My throat would literally feel like it closed. The depression was severe. I was trapped in steady mind traffic. I would plan how to get back at the people who hurt me or how to end my life. All kinds of phobias set in. Claustrophobia and agoraphobia, to name a few. Life, to me, was a living hell.

I would beg God to help me, and I promised I would do better if He did. I tried, but I could not sustain change for very long. As I began this new journey with the Lord, I started dealing with symptoms and emotions of the past that alarmed me. It signaled to me it was coming up for healing! Thank you, God; I have the answer to freedom, YOU!

Be encouraged, Beloved. We do not have to be ashamed of issues that come up for us. Jesus knows our deepest thoughts and understands the secret longings of our hearts. He endures our pain alongside us. He loves us and wants us to run to Him so that He can free us.

Heb 4:15

> *"For we do not have a high priest who is unable to empathize with our weaknesses, but we have one who has been tempted in every way, just as we are—yet he did not sin."*

He identifies with us. There is nothing that shocks Him. I love that about Him. It means we can talk to Him about ANYTHING. He is always there for us. (Psalm 139:2)

So, I started talking with Him about all that anger, fear, rejection, and the like. I desperately needed His help. He led me to these scriptures that were written miraculously and specifically for me (or so I thought). This is the Truth, and this truth has set me free.

Gal 5:20-22

> *"Then there is the worshiping of a distorted image of one-self which is what idolatry is all about; drugs, hatred, constant conflict, jealous suspicion, violent outbursts of rage, everyone for himself in a cut-throat competitive world, trampling on others to get to the top, dissension, heresy, and manipulating people's minds with false teachings. (the flesh is not your lower nature, it is the fruit of the "I-am-not-tree-system; it is a mind-set governed by a sense of lack and desperately trying to do life by sheer will power, independent of your Source)*

This is such a sad picture of a life consumed with envious self-pity, murder, drunken stupor, intoxicated licentiousness, and lust, with all the quarrels and jealousies it ignites. As I have stated before, those who practice this lifestyle have nothing in common with the Kingdom of God or our inheritance in Him. (The authority of the Christ-life opposes and defeats the dominance of the flesh)

Spirit effortlessly bears the rich harvest of love, joy, peace, patience, kindness, goodness, integrity, gentleness, and self-control; all these individually reveal the irresistible attraction of the inner life of our design. (They are not fading, fragile emotions produced by willpower. This is the fruit of what you know in your spirit to be true about you. Fruit is the effortless, spontaneous expression of the character of the tree. Rest in the awareness and assurance of who you really are!)

There I was – splayed out for all to see - right in scripture! The distorted image I had of myself was idolatry. Lies of the whisperer, Satan, that brought deception. The false identity imagined in my mind and living in that illusion. There is the fruit, the out-of-control emotions, and the behavior I was experiencing. Any image that is not the image and likeness of our authentic self is a distortion of the genuine.

Yikes, ugly and precisely what I experienced.

Yes, this is a sad way and unnecessary way to live. I was deceived into thinking I was in control of my life. The truth is, I was being controlled. Then, I awakened to my union in Christ.

The critical failure here is doing life on our own without God. It is also contrary to the very nature He put in us. The Word of God will set us free from being ruled by the sense realm. It will correct the corrupt and distorted image of ourselves, along with the distortion of our thoughts and emotions. He has set us free to live our true inner life of the spirit.

Heb 4:12

The message of God spoke to us in Christ, is the most life giving and dynamic influence in us, cutting like a surgeon's scalpel, sharper than a soldier's sword, piercing to the deepest core of human conscience, to the dividing of soul and spirit, ending the dominance of the sense realm and its neutralizing effect upon the human spirit. In this way a person's spirit is freed tobecome the ruling influence again in the thoughts and intensions of their heart. The scrutiny of this living Sword-Logos detects every possible disease, discerning the body's deepest secrets where joint and bone-marrow meet."

Say goodbye to guilt, inferiority, shame, and sin-consciousness (distorted thinking) and all the fruit of that distorted images' behavior. The Grace of God set us free.

Gal 6:2-4

> *"The law of the Christ-life distinguishes your spirituality; taking the weight off someone's shoulder is fulfilling the law of Christ. (The message of Grace removes all law-related burdens such as guilt, suspicion, inferiority, shame and a sin-consciousness.) Anyone who imagines to be someone they are not, lives a lie. (The law system sponsors pretense; grace reveals your true identity redeemed in Christ.) Now, without the pressure of pretense, you are free to give expression to your individual self and not some phony life you're trying to fake."*

Acknowledging who Jesus is, grace awakens us to our authentic selves and inner life. He rescues us from being someone we are not and living a phony life.

Forgiven and set free from a lifestyle that misses the mark of our true life in Christ. A life lived from the spirit within us. The inner, authentic, and genuine life.

Contact! That is the AH HA moment that makes every moment of our life worth living.

See that? The Spirit of God in our spirit reveals to us what we know in our spirit to be true about us.

Gal 2:20

> *"So here I am dead and alive at the same time! I'm dead to the old me I was trying to be and alive to the real me which is Christ in me! I was in him in his death; now he is in me in my life! For the first time I'm free to be me in my skin, immersed in his faith in our joint sonship! He loves me and believes in me! He is God's gift to me."*

Then I discover I am dead to the old, distorted image, lies, deception, and expression of that distortion. We are dead to expressing destructive emotions rooted in the distorted image. I am now alive to the real me, which is Christ in me. Free to be me in my skin. Loved and accepted by God.

Our emotions are not only good; they are valid and God-given. After all, we are made in His image. The Lord led me to a myriad of scriptures that showed me a very expressive Jesus. I love to discover who He is and be able to identify with Him. He is passionate and compassionate just like me! He laughs and cries. He gets angry at injustice; He is joyful and peaceful. He dances and sings. In other words, He is a person that experiences feelings and expresses them just like we do.

Heb 4:15

"Jesus was touched with the feeling of our infirmities"

He identifies with us but does not leave us in that distorted and defeated place. He victoriously faced every onslaught we could ever encounter, which enabled us to expect this same victory! We are empowered to enforce victory and master everything - including our negative emotions.

Mat 9:36

"When He saw the crowds, He was moved with compassion and pity for them, because they were dispirited and distressed, like sheep without a shepherd."

Pain, suffering, grief, and anxiety are what we experience when we violate our identity. Joy is the name we give to the experience of living in sync with the life of the Father, Son, and Spirit. Sorrow is the name we give to the experience of living in violation of that life. The cause of the breach may have come internally or externally, but it hurts so profoundly, whatever the reason. It disturbs us because it violates our "being," and our spirit experiences this acutely.

Jesus is known for His compassion. He rescues, delivers, and heals lives – still. That same Jesus reaches His heart and hand to you now. You can choose to say, "Yes, Jesus, I receive your love." Expect your transformation!

Chapter 10

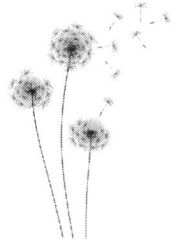

His Way is the Way!

I always thought my way was right. I wanted my way, and my opinion was always correct. I did not trust anyone; therefore, I fought to be in control at all costs.

However, my inner turmoil always created chaos instead of control. I ended up losing every time. In contrast, as I chose God's thoughts and ways, my outcomes were profitable and healing.

Prov 14:12

> *"There is a way which seems right to a man, but its end is the way of death."*

I could give many examples of this principle, but I think you are getting the idea at this point in the book. Living life His way assures you an abundant life. Now it is a matter of learning to stop and listen to His guidance. The more you practice this principle, the more fruit you will see. Make a point to develop that beautiful relationship with time, meditation, and prayer. As we stated the following scripture previously, it is worth repeating right here:

John 10:10

> *"The thief comes only in order to steal and kill and destroy. I came that they may have and enjoy life, and have it in abundance (to the full, till it overflows)."*

I will elaborate a little about the "thief" referred to in that verse. The "thief" is Satan. This evil spirit is the "voice of lies" that distorts your image and thoughts. His voice always leads to deception about oneself and God. Soon, we begin to identify its false realities versus the Truth, and we are instantly delivered from its devastating blows. My spiritual mentor taught me a powerful lesson many years ago that serves me well to this day. Scrutinize your thoughts -especially if they are causing you some internal dissonance. If something doesn't "feel right" in your spirit, ask your spirit if this thought is likely from God or Satan. The answer should be obvious - but get in the habit of verifying this answer with God, the Truth.

What does God say about this situation? Take captive all contrary thoughts and subject them to the Truth. This results in instant revelation and protection. We can do this because of what He has already accomplished on the Cross. The following scripture is known widely as the "suffering servant" – Jesus.

Jesus already accomplished our Healing…

Isa 53:5

> *"But He was wounded for our transgressions, He was crushed for our wickedness [our sin, our injustice, our wrongdoing]; The punishment [required] for our well-being fell on Him, And by His stripes (wounds) we are healed."*

How did Jesus' death prevent our misfortune and offer us healing? After the fall of humankind in the Garden, we began to live with a distorted reality of our "image." The original sin was essentially an "identity crisis" offered by Satan. We required restoration like a '57 Chevy! Jesus came as a perfect man to redeem us from that "identity" death trap. He died for our imperfections by absorbing them into himself.

He experienced all the sickness, disease, and death a human could experience, redeeming us to our original image and likeness of God.

God is our hope…

The "God kind of hope" means to anticipate with pleasure, have confidence, and have faith in good things to come – simply because He loves us. He has put His love in our hearts so we can confidently expect abundance.

Rom 5:5

> *"Such hope never disappoints or deludes or shames us, for God's love has been poured out in our hearts through the Holy Spirit Who has been given to us."*

Who in this world has not been betrayed and disappointed from time to time in our lives? Sometimes this is due to false expectations and sometimes due to misunderstandings. Too often, I discovered the disappointment was due to my inferior motivations. I was trying to get my needs met through people versus God. His superior motive is Love. He has never disappointed me when I put my trust in Him.

Eph 2:8

> *"And He raised us up together with Him (when we believed), and He did this so that in the ages to come He might clearly show the immeasurable and unsurpassed riches of His grace in His kindness towards us in Christ Jesus by providing for our redemption."*

God eagerly wants to shower us with His loving kindness and release His provision into our lives. He restored us to participate in our divine origin and escape the distorted influence of corruption. He already raised us up together with Him.

Humanity must awaken to this immeasurable gift.

When our expectation is in God, he does not disappoint us because He is love. He is the true love we have always been looking for.

This Godly hope is unlike saying, 'I wish it could happen.' This kind of hope is an 'earnest expectation' of Him. We are looking to be provided for by Him and experience our completeness in Him. He is the one that does not disappoint.

People may let us down, but God does not. He is the provision that we need in every situation. Allow Him to infuse you.

Col 2:29

"For in Him all the fullness of Deity (the Godhead) dwells in bodily form [completely expressing the divine essence of God]."

The Godhead dwells in you and me. The Godhead can't be and do anything other than who They are and what They do. The Godhead is in us, and we express Their nature in our personality.

Col 2:10

"And in Him you have been made complete [achieving spiritual stature through Christ], and He is the head over all rule and authority [of every angelic and earthly power]."

The full measure of everything God has in mind for you and me has been completed. He is in us! Our completeness is realized and experienced in Him. We are protected and are One with Him. Our job is to actualize this fact on this earth so that all may recognize this Truth.

John 17:21

"That they all may be one, [just] as You, Father, are in Me and I in You, that they also may be one in Us, so that the world may believe and be convinced that You have sent Me."

Take a moment—center on Him in your spirit. Know you are not alone, and all that He is dwells in you. You are inseparable, complete and completely loved. You are one with Him.

Chapter 11

A New Creation in Christ...

We have become a new creation through what Jesus did for us. What does this mean? To answer this, let's begin with what God said He accomplished for us.

II Cor. 5:17 (Mirror)

> *"Now, in the light of your co-inclusion in his death and resurrection, whoever you thought you were before, in Christ you are a brand-new person! The old ways of seeing yourself and everyone else are over. Acquaint yourself with the new!"*

That's what we purpose to do by renewing our minds according to what God says. It is an awakening that happens through Truth on a deeper level than mere intellectual or academic learning.

Our minds need to be saved and infused with the life of God. In other words, we need our minds washed with the Truth.

Eph 4:23

> *"...and be continually renewed in the spirit of your mind [having a fresh, untarnished mental and spiritual attitude],"*

This renewal will cause you to be positively re-programmed in how you think about yourself! As we grow in our awareness of being made in His image, likeness, and oneness, we become influenced and guided by Him more and more. That's what being renewed in the spirit will do. We see with new spiritual eyes and therefore act accordingly.

I kept seeking. My Spirit continued to awaken to the Truth of who God is and who I am in Him.

Col 3:1-2

> *"Therefore, if you have been raised with Christ [to a new life, sharing in His resurrection from the dead], keep seeking the things that are above, where Christ is, seated at the right hand of God. Set your mind and keep focused habitually on the things above [the heavenly things], not on things that are on the earth [which have only temporal value]."*

We are mentally relocating as we engage our thoughts with throne room realities. What is a throne room reality and how do we relocate there? This mental "place" is where we are when we actualize being raised with Christ (resurrected). We fill our minds with the Word of God and practice seeing ourselves as God sees us. The temptation is to be distracted with the earthly soul-ruled realm. Instead, focus on seeing things from above, from His perspective. Meditate on being in that throne room, in the heavenlies, with Him!

Interesting quote by Frances Du Toit: "A renewed mind conquers the space previously occupied by worthless pursuits and habits."

Child of God, not only will He work all things for your good because He loves you, but we also never have to go around the same mountain of destruction again. We are set free to experience Christ's life in total dominion and in union with love, Himself.

We have choices! Let's not let the illusion of the old life control us! Choose life!

Roms 8:28

> *"We are assured and know that [[a]God being a partner in their labor] all things work together and are [fitting into a plan] for good to and for those who love God and are called according to [His] design and purpose."*

Let's partner with Him by thinking like Him.

Transformation by the Renewing of Your Mind...

The Word of God says, meditate on who God is, who I am in Him, and I will find and see myself. That is just the start of the more wonderful things He provided for us. I had to "choose" to believe this!

Did my entire thinking and life change immediately? No. Did applying His word change my life entirely? Yes! I have learned that a relationship with God is just downright practical. In fact, I was not interested in believing in a God that was not relative and relatable to my life, in the here and now!

My mind was so warped and deluded that when people tried to talk with me, I often missed what they were trying to convey altogether. My personal transformation took a while to sink in. The dialog of lies and deception that was going on in my mind was loud and distracting. As I received more Truth, these inferior thoughts began to fade. It took an intentional application of the Truth to get free. I wanted to change and believed God's truth would free me.

Again, God's Word proved to be true. On a practical level, I began to ask the Holy Spirit to highlight or clarify what I had missed while 'listening' to another speak to me. I apologized for being distracted and focused more intently. By doing that, I allowed the Holy Spirit to expose the illusions and grids that were twisting my understanding – just like when my father misunderstood MY words!

I am profoundly grateful that the stronghold of delusion has been defeated in my life! Clarity has replaced confusion because now I listen with my heart as I partner with Holy Spirit. Now, I am able to interact with people by my authentic spirit life, which translates into healing for them and for me! Hallelujah -The journey continues!

The Mirror translation, for me, gives the most accurate translation of what it means to be transformed by renewing our minds. This concept is life-changing for anyone who chooses to believe Him.

Rom 12:1-2

> *"Live consistent with who you really are, inspired by the loving kindness of God. My brothers, the most practical expression of worship is to make your bodies available to him as a living sacrifice; this pleases him more than any religious routine. He desires to find visible, individual expression in your person. Do not allow current religious tradition to mold you into its pattern of reasoning. Like an inspired artist, give attention to the detail of God's desire to find expression in you. Become acquainted with perfection. To accommodate yourself to the delight and good pleasure of him will transform your thoughts afresh from within."*

Practically speaking – Let You Be You! Don't discourage or compare yourself to anyone else. Be thoroughly and genuinely pleased with who He made you to be and refresh yourself in His love! Express the God in you!

Sin, The Fallen Mindset...

Let's talk about what most religions seem to dwell on, and then let's conquer it with Jesus! What is sin? The word "sin" in Greek is the word "hamartia." It connotes "living without your allotted portion or without form, pointing to a disorientated, distorted, bankrupt identity." To live in sin is to live out of context with the blueprint of one's design, to behave out of tune with God's original harmony. Naturally, you'll see that my favorite translation regarding this intimidating concept is from the Mirror: Essentially, sin is nothing more than distorted behavior caused by an identity warp. This is a revelation that will transform you..

I John 3:4-9

> *"Distorted behavior is the result of a warped self-image! A lost sense of identity is the basis of all sin! Sin's source is a fallen mindset, from the beginning! For this purpose, the Son of God was revealed! His mission was to undo the works of the Devil! To discover one's authentic sonship in God, is to discover true freedom from sin. We are born of him and his seed remains in us; this is the only possible reference to sober up the mind from the intoxicating influence of deception."*

I started thinking about God's thoughts. We must begin living from our God identity, not the fallen mindset. Free from the intoxications of deception, we sober up in our minds and start to experience the superior life of our design in Him. We are God's authentic Sons and Daughters; we should act and think like it.

God Saved and Forgave Us...

The Bible says we were dead in our sins.

Eph 2:1 (NLT)

> *"Once you were dead because of your disobedience and your many sins."*

This state of mind is where I was when I found God. I was dead. (he never lost me, but I certainly lost me). I was in a death trap of an inferior lifestyle, constantly living below the blueprint measure of my life. I pray this is not where you are; can you relate on some level in your life with this? I am delighted to share that it does not have to be this way.

Jesus shed His Blood and bore in His body all the disfigurement of a distorted image to heal us. He set us free and has FORGIVEN us from past choices and the consequences of those choices. Living an inferior lifestyle is not for us. We are to live as Kings and Priests, Sons and Daughters, and Heirs to the Throne – Free as a bird. This statement should be the most excellent news for anyone *spiritually* dead.

Psa 103:12

> *"As far as the east is from the west, so far has He removed our transgressions from us."*

Transformation...

When shall we be transformed? When we believe this:

I John 4:17 (Mirror)

> *"Our confident conversation echoes this fellowship even in the face of crisis; because as He is, so are we in this world- our lives are mirrored in Him. We are as blameless in this life as Jesus is! This perfect love union is the source of our confidence whenever we face the scrutiny of contradiction."*

All contradictions to the above statement will tempt us to question and doubt the truth. Please don't fall for it. Simply readjust your focus. Peace is a good indicator of our focus. Do we have conflict, or do we have peace? Peace, of course, is Him.

Peace, marvelous, priceless, peace is available for you and me. It surpasses all understanding. The ancient Hebrew concept of peace, "Shalom," meant wholeness, completeness, soundness, health, safety, and prosperity. Shalom. Nothing is missing, nothing broken. All of Mankind seeks this peace, and Truth is, it is available in Him. The Peacemaker. Just ask Him and receive it.

Phil 4:6-7 Amp.

> *"Do not fret or have any anxiety about anything, but in every circumstance and in everything, by prayer and petition (definite requests), with thanksgiving, continue to make your wants known to God. And God's peace [shall be yours, that a tranquil state of a soul assured of its salvation through Christ, and so fearing nothing from God and being content with its earthly lot of whatever sort that is, that peace] which transcends all understanding shall garrison and mount guard over your hearts and minds in Christ Jesus."*

Who is this Peacemaker?

When I think of the Peacemaker, I envision Jesus when He was transfigured on the Mount of Sinai, perhaps because this is how He appeared to me when He showed me His peace. What a spectacular moment that must have been!

Matt 17:1-2

> *"Six days later, Jesus took with Him Peter and James, and his brother John, and led them up on a high mountain by themselves. And He was transfigured before them; and His face shone like the sun, and His garments became as white as light…"*

What I want to point out about this passage is, The Holy Spirit reveals Jesus to His disciples for who He is. The Holy Spirit tells us what He hears the Father saying and reveals Jesus to us.

Remember my story of that "light" that showed up and delivered me from my deadly habit of drinking? That "light" that shone around me was brighter than the afternoon sun. I had an awakening and encounter with who Jesus is, and I was instantly healed and peaceful. From then on, I had an insatiable appetite to know Him. This spectacular moment of Truth was powerful and loving and was revealed to me by the Holy Spirit. Anybody who believes that this transfiguring moment is available for them can receive it! I am writing this book so that you, too, can have the "light" go on in you. What He did for me, He will do for you. Anything is possible with God. You are never too far gone. He meets you in your darkest place and brings you out into the *light*.

He invites you, saying: "I am shining My Light in your heart, revealing Myself to you. I am the One drawing you. I am the lifter of your head. Look into My face of love, for you; see your reflection in My face."

Matt 16:15

> *"He said to them, "But who do you say that I am?" Simon Peter replied, "You are the Christ (the Messiah, the Anointed), the Son of the living God. Then Jesus answered him, "Blessed [happy, spiritually secure, favored by God] are you, Simon son of Jonah, because flesh and blood (mortal man) did not reveal this to you, but My Father who is in heaven."*

You are secure, and Father in heaven is revealing Himself to you. The bigger question, at this point, is, "Who do You Say You are?"

Let God Tell You!

I John 3:1-2 Mirror

"Consider the amazing love the Father lavished upon us; this is our defining moment: we began in the agape of God-the engineer of the universe is our Father! So it's no wonder that the performance-based systems of this world just cannot see this! Because they do not recognize their origin in God, they feel indifferent towards anyone who does! Beloved, we know that we are children of God to begin with, which means that there can be no future surprises; his manifest likeness is already mirrored in us! Our sameness cannot be compromised or contradicted; our gaze will confirm exactly who he is-and who we are."

We are born of love, as His child. We are innocent, forgiven, secure, justified, glorified, whole, sound, healthy, and prosperous. We are the overcoming free ones! And that, beloved, just skims the surface!

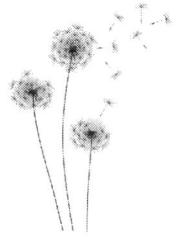

Chapter 12
Glorious and Wonderful Holy Spirit...

We are not alone…

John 14:16-17,26-27

> *"And I will ask the Father, and He will give you another [a]Helper (Comforter, Advocate, Intercessor—Counselor, Strengthener, Standby), to be with you forever— the Spirit of Truth, whom the world cannot receive [and take to its heart] because it does not see Him or know Him, but you know Him because He (the Holy Spirit) remains with y o u continually and will be in you. "I have told you these things while I am still with you. 26 But the [b]Helper (Comforter, Advocate, Intercessor—Counselor, Strengthener, Standby), the Holy Spirit, whom the Father will send in My name [in My place, to represent Me and act on My behalf], He will teach you all things. And He will help you remember every-thing that I have told you. 27 Peace I leave with you; My [perfect] peace I give to you; not as the world gives do I give to you. Do not let your heart be troubled, nor let it be afraid. [Let My perfect peace calm you in every circumstance and give you courage and strength for every challenge.]"*

The Spirit of Truth is our Eternal companion. He reminds us of our authentic identity. He is our intimate companion, never to leave or forsake us. He is the giver of peace, com-forter, advocate, intercessor, counselor, strengthener, stand-by, and helper. He is in you and I forever.

He is the best friend that our hearts have always desired. He is faithful, joyful, compassionate, understanding, and protective. He is loyal and has our back. He is with us always in everything we do. He is so personal and personable. He is the revealer of Jesus Christ.

His immediate presence continues to be one with us. We are never alone. Our whole being is flooded with comfort, and the feeling of completeness floods us the moment we put our attention on Him. Even when we don't 'feel' Him, we know that we are inseparable, and nothing will separate us from him.

How could we ask for anything more?

Only Father, Son, and Holy Spirit could come up with this most brilliant plan and implement it.

Rom 8:28,29

> *"For I am convinced [and continue to be convinced—beyond any doubt] that neither death, nor life, nor angels, nor principalities, nor things present and threatening, nor things to come, nor powers, nor height, nor depth, nor any other created thing, will be able to separate us from the [unlimited] love of God, which is in Christ Jesus our Lord."*

Nothing, Beloved has, can, or ever will separate you and me from His love. Not sin. Not delusion. Not death. It is only an illusion, a deception, that would cause you to think you are separated from Him. The Incarnation, death, burial, resurrection, ascension, and enthronement of Jesus Christ is our assurance of our union.

Sending His Holy Spirit to dwell in us is the tangible proof and guarantee of His eternal love. These facts are a non-negotiable Truth. Believing in Him is when we experience the Truth. It is true, whether we believe it or not. It is life-giving when we do. I know.

Being Led by the Holy Spirit...

Holy Spirit guides us into the truth by communicating and unveiling that what is true about Jesus is also true about us. Holy Spirit gives us the heavenly reality within us and leads us into that experience.

He wants to be involved and helpful in our everyday life and relationships. This is His expertise directly from the Father.

John 16:13

> *"But when He, the Spirit of Truth, comes, He will guide you into all the truth [full and complete truth]. For He will not speak on His own initiative,   but He will speak whatever He hears [from the Father—the message regarding the Son], and He will disclose to you what is to come [in the future]."*

Any decision – whether paying bills, deciding where to work, buying, exercising, or simply relaxing should be done with input from our best friend, the Holy Spirit.

He is brilliant and will guide you well. I will give you a personal experience.

Years ago, I was taking classes to learn about real estate investments - doing fixes and flips of homes just out of enjoyment and perhaps to make some extra money. About a year into it, the Holy Spirit spoke to my heart about getting my real estate license. I was so surprised. I was always interested in the design and architecture of homes, and I thoroughly enjoyed looking at the interiors. When I heard Him speak that to me, I was a salon owner and hairdresser of 38 years. I never considered making a change, nor did I have the confidence to think I could pass the test to get a license. Holy Spirit put that desire in my heart and led me to enroll in the appropriate real estate school. After eight years of being in my career change, I am now considering adding the staging aspect of real estate. I believe the Holy Spirit will reveal more to me, and I am eager to discover my potential. It is beautiful to be led by the most brilliant mind in the universe!

The Holy Spirit can also warn you of future dangers or circumstances. I have lost count of the invaluable protective dreams I have had. He always led me to an excellent outcome!

Once, the Holy Spirit gave me a dream about being interrogated while entering a foreign country. He showed me the whole process of this frightening experience, including the conversation, my baggage search, and the outcome. Years later, I went on a mission trip to a foreign country, and the exact scenario happened as he showed me. I responded to the questions precisely as the Holy Spirit reminded me in the dream. I was at ease in the face of intimidating circumstances because the Holy Spirit had already assured me of the excellent outcome.

I had another protective warning dream. I lived alone in a small condo complex. Holy Spirit warned me of a 'peeping tom' in my dream. I woke up and prayed in my spirit language and my native English language. One afternoon, I was hosting a prayer meeting at my home. There were about 15 of us praying and worshipping the Lord. That same evening my neighbor told me of seeing a man peeping through the back kitchen window, and she confronted him. He ran off. He got to see and hear 15 people praying and worshipping God. I believe that was a Holy Spirit setup, and God had quite an impact on that person!

You have much to look forward to in your relationship with Holy Spirit.

Rom 8:14

"For all who are led by the Spirit of God are sons of God."

Life is so rich with the Holy Spirit. It is so comforting to know He leads us into a meaningful and overcoming life here on earth. Mirror Translation puts it this way.

Rom 8:13-14

"In light of all this, to now continue to live under the sinful influence of the senses, is to reinstate the dominion of spiritual death. Instead, we are indebted to now exhibit the highest expression of life inspired by the Spirit. This life demonstrated zero tolerance to the habits and sinful patterns of the flesh. The original life of the Father revealed in his Son is the life the Spirit now conducts with us."

This life is the one that God has always lovingly intended for us. Think of that!

Following the Holy Spirit's lead brings us to maturity. The influence of our senses does not dominate us. Our character starts to reflect Jesus more and more. It is deeply gratifying not to react out of emotion but to respond to challenges maturely and by choice.

As we discussed in my previous life, I believed God was ready to lower the boom on me whenever I messed up. I had a victim mentality and behaved like one. As a result, I was volatile, unstable in all my ways, destructive, and just downright bitter and resentful. Now, I know that Jesus set us free from the dominion of the law of performance. (Gal.5:18 Amp.)

When we are tempted by our emotions to live a life without God's love, we naturally will lose, living way below our standard of life in Christ. We must learn to express His love in us to become victorious.

Results of the Leadership of the Holy Spirit...

Being led by the Holy Spirit has been a transformational, life-giving change for me. I can guarantee it is for anyone else, also.

Gal 5:22-26 Amp

> *"But the fruit of the Spirit [the result of His presence within us] is love [unselfish concern for others], joy, [inner] peace, patience [not the ability to wait, but how we act while waiting], kindness, goodness, faithfulness, gentleness, self-control. Against such things, there is no law. But the fruit of being led by the Holy Spirit, from Him living within us is freedom."*

We can not only face difficult people and situations, but Holy Spirit will help us navigate through whatever problem we may encounter in overcoming victory. The spirit of God will help us respond from our superior inner reality of who we are in Christ. We will be known for displaying the character and nature of God within us during and through our trials.

Once, I had a challenging and hurtful situation in which a person lied about me to my business and church community, all the while pretending to be my friend.

Naturally, I felt betrayed, and I got angry. I was exasperated to the point of exhibiting mental and physical symptoms. I couldn't sleep well while trying to justify my emotions of exacting physical revenge. I finally asked the Lord for His wisdom and to help me! He said to go to the person and ask for forgiveness. I said, 'You want me to do what??!!' I was not happy about this advice. I went on to tell Him this: 'By the way, Lord, If you haven't noticed, I'm the one hurt here and being attacked. Why would he turn this situation around to the point where I was apologizing for their lie? It just didn't make sense. I prayed for the right heart attitude and the courage to do what He was leading me to do. I saw the wisdom of why and the possibility that I may have hurt this person. I did what He said.

I went to this person and said, I realize what is going on, and I asked for forgiveness for anything I did that may have hurt this person. This person denied what was being said and lied to me. Well. This scenario surely didn't look like I thought it would since I obeyed His guidance. In fact, it got worse when the person got furious with me for bringing it up. The Lord told me to keep quiet and not to defend myself. He would take care of the situation. I held my tongue and forgave this person.

Over the next year, I got healed, and my reputation was restored. It was a valuable lesson in controlling my emotional temptation to retaliate by leaning into the Holy Spirit instead. I was empowered to turn my anger and fear into compassion and forgiveness. The conclusion was victorious and powerful.

God freed me again! I'm guessing you might have had a similar experience in your lifetime. I pray this example enlightens your solutions for freedom as well!

Do I do it all right by the spirit every time? No. He understands and gives us the grace to overcome when we miss it. Thankfully, the times of allowing the natural to dominate and control me, to my detriment, have gotten less and less. I prefer living the spirited lifestyle and the freedom gained from appropriating our true identity in Him.

Eph. 3:16

> *"May He grant you out of the riches of His glory, to be strengthened and spiritually energized with power through His Spirit in your inner self, [indwelling your innermost being and personality]"*

Our strength is in Him. He spiritually energizes us with His power to face and overcome anything. Truly, victory is sweet!

Rom 8:37

> *"Yet in all these things we are more than conquerors and gain an overwhelming victory through Him who loved us [so much that He died for us]."*

You are "more than a conqueror" in Him, who loves you. Victory in everything is yours.

II Cor 3:17

> *"Now the Lord is the Spirit, and where the Spirit of the Lord is, there is liberty (emancipation from bondage, freedom)."*

You live in Him, in freedom.

In plain language, God says, "Allow me to show you how to live a superior lifestyle. Come into the plan I originally had for you from the beginning."

Col 3:25 Mirror

> *"To live contrary to the life of your design is to injure yourself;..."* Living in sync with your authentic self in harmony with God is loving yourself. **We are One with Him...**

Being a co-member of the body of Christ, we are joined to the Lord in His death, burial, resurrection, ascension, and enthronement. We are joint heirs, and possessors, with Him.

I Cor 6:17

> *"But the one who is united and joined to the Lord is one spirit with Him."*

We are the express image of Him in a human body. We are joined in all He has accomplished. That was the promise.

I Cor 12:27

> *"Do you not know that your body is a temple of the Holy Spirit who is within you, whom you have [received as a gift] from God, and that you are not your own [property]?"*

We exist because of Him, solely.

Acts 17:28

> *"For in Him we live and move and exist [that is, in Him we actually have our being], as even some of [a]your poets have said, 'For we also are His children."*

We are co-laboring with Him to expand and increase our abundant life here and now. This life is to be realized on this earth realm NOW – not just in a future "heaven." We are already in "heaven" because the Kingdom of God is within us!

Luke 17:21

> *"We live simultaneously in the Kingdom of God on the earth."*

Don't fall for the 'big lie' that we need to escape the earth, die, and go to heaven to live the life God has planned for us. We are complete NOW! We are complete and lack nothing in Him…

Col 2:9-11 (Mirror)

> *"In him, all the fullness of Deity resides in a human body! He proves that human life is tailor-made for God! We are complete in Him! Jesus mirrors our wholeness and endorses*

our true identity. He is "I am" in us! We are complete and whole, in Him. Shalom, Nothing missing, nothing broken! You were in Christ when he died, which means that his death is your true circumcision."

This co-being is not hypothetical; this is the real deal. Sin's authority in the human body was stripped of its control over you. Remember, the deception distracts you and tries to get you to believe your needs are not met. It is an illusion with superficial, temporary fixes as an answer. We start to seek for what we already have. That evil power was defeated of its control over us. Don't exchange the truth for the lie that you are not complete!

It is a simple adjustment. Pause; look within; put your eyes on the Truth and in the Word of God. Ah, there He is, your all and all. Once we see the truth we become at rest; we no longer look and demand others to be what they cannot be nor were designed to be for us. No more, out on our own to fend for ourselves, only to be disappointed with the superficial, temporary fixes of this earthly realm.

Chapter 13

We Are in Possession Because of Our Position...

We are not limited to what the current worldly facts are concerning our lives. Our spiritual inheritance is all that truly matters. We already possess what Jesus obtained for us. We have been rescued from control and relocated in the Abundant life of Christ.

Col 1:12-13 (Mirror)

> *"We are grateful to the Father who qualified us to participate in the complete portion of the inheritance of the saints in the light. He rescued us from the dominion of darkness and relocated us into the kingdom where the love of his Son rules."*

We are His children, the inheritors of all that Jesus ransomed for us. His Holy Spirit is the guarantee of our inheritance.

Rom 8:17

> *"Because we are his offspring, we qualify to be heirs; God Himself is our portion, we co-inherit with Christ. Since we were represented and included in his suffering we equally participate in the glory of his resurrection."*

Col 3:24

> *"Knowing [with all certainty] that it is from the Lord [not from men] that you will receive the inheritance which is your [greatest] reward. It is the Lord Christ whom you [actually] serve."*

Eph 1:14 (Mirror)

> *"The Holy Spirit is our tangible link to the inheritance that was ransomed and preserved for us. God's glorious plan for mankind is theme of our celebration."*

What does it mean that the Holy Spirit is the guarantor of our inheritance? The word "guarantee" comes from the Hebrew word, meaning to braid, as two parties intertwine by giving something as surety and pledge. The pledge represents the full transaction. The legal document or title deed represents the entire value of a transaction. It is much like a wedding ring representing the completeness of a love union.

The unveiled logic of God has been revealed to you now. The Trinity gave the surety and pledge in our Better New Covenant (Hebrews). He has sealed us; He is in us and He guarantees our inheritance in the Covenant. There is nothing more superior.

The earth is our inheritance...

Ps. 2:7-8

> *"I have given you the ends of the earth as your inheritance. The Lord created the earth for us! It is His gift."*

This Truth that the earth is your inheritance should give you purpose and freedom, now. This is our permission to "leave behind" the escapist mentality popular from the last few centuries. We do not have to get air-vac'd out of this earth to experience all that heaven has for us. God's original purpose in giving us this earth for our inheritance was not a temporary stay.

Let's read in scripture what God intended us to do with this earth. Like Adam and Eve, we are to fill the earth with the blessing we are blessed with. He has a purpose and supplies us with everything we need to fulfill the plan.

Gen 1:26-28

> *"God said, Let Us [Father, Son, and Holy Spirit] make mankind in Our image, after Our likeness, and let them have complete authority over the fish of the sea, the birds of the air, the [tame] beasts, and over all of the earth, and over everything that creeps upon the earth. So, God created man in His own image, in the image and likeness of God He created him; male and female He created them. And God blessed them and said to them, Be fruitful, multiply, and fill the earth, and subdue it [using all its vast resources in the service of God and man]; and have dominion over the fish of the sea, the birds of the air, and over every living creature that moves upon the earth."*

Does that sound like a temporary plan? No. This mandate is who we are and what we do - forever. We shall experience life from our authentic selves - with purpose. We will experience the co-ascension of life with God – "on earth as it is in heaven."

The Sons and daughters of God are to take dominion over this earth, governing all of creation for the restoration of all things. (Acts 3:21) We are to reign and rule into existence the finished work of Jesus. (Romans 5:17) We are empowered to live the victorious life because of Jesus Christ.

Can you believe God created us to co-labor with Him in His Wisdom and Creativity to subdue this earth - eternally?

Wow, mind-expanding, isn't it! All of creation is waiting for us to bring them into their freedom.

Rom 8:21

> *"All creation knows that the glorious liberty of the sons of God sets the stage for their own release from decay."*

We will set free all of creation from decay and corruption, agony and pain, and restore it to its former intended glory.

The Kingdom of God is within you. We govern into existence heaven on earth, the Garden of Eden restored and expanded! You are heaven on earth. God's original plan is made possible through Jesus; what was lost is now recovered.

Sons and daughters of God, THIS is our destiny and our purpose for eternity!

Isaiah 9:7

> *"Of the increase of His government and of peace there shall be no end, upon the throne of David and over his kingdom, to establish it and to uphold it with justice and with righteousness from the [latter] time forth, even forevermore. The zeal of the Lord of hosts will perform this."*

There is no end to experiencing the fruit of His labor. The Kingdom of God is limitless. Eternally, our purpose is to rule and reign in this life with Jesus - in love.

Chapter 14
See Where You Are Located...

Are we on earth, or are we in heaven? Are we in a fortress or a dungeon? Are we in mental agony or bliss?

Col 3:1-4 (mirror)

> *"See yourselves co-raised with Christ! Now ponder with persuasion the consequence of your co-inclusion in him. Relocate yourselves mentally! Engage your thoughts with throne room realities where you are co-seated with Christ in the executive authority of God's right hand. Becoming affectionately acquainted with throne room thoughts will keep you from being distracted again by the earthly (soul-ruled) realm. (Set your minds upon the things that are above and not upon the things below -RSV) Your union with his death broke the association with that world; see yourselves located in a fortress where your life is hidden with Christ in God! The unveiling of Christ, as defining our lives, immediately implies that, what is evident in him, is equally mirrored in you! The exact life on exhibit in Christ is now repeated in us. We are included in the same bliss and joined oneness with Him; just as his life reveals you, your life reveals him."*

When we look at Him, we see ourselves. His spirit resonates within our spirit to confirm that we originate in God. Whatever we face daily, we are to acquaint ourselves with the greater reality. The earthly soul-ruled realm is irrelevant to us. The unseen eternal realm within us has our full attention and captivates our gaze! We are the ones in dominion.

It just takes an instant to see the Truth, like a twinkling of an eye. One moment we can feel inferior, and the next, we can engage our thoughts with Truth and instantly feel and act out of our greater reality. He made us wonderfully. It's that simple. Let us reboot our minds with Truth by focusing on Him. The earth realm is always in competition for our thought life. As we affectionately communicate with God, our thoughts gladly respond supernaturally.

We start to identify with who we are because it is our True nature. We watch old things we have felt and done naturally fall away. There is no desire to drink or do drugs excessively; lie; be bitter; or any number of former sinful behaviors because it is not our true nature to do so. When there is a wrong desire, we now innately realize that it is contrary to our makeup, and we have the inner power to overcome it. In reality, we have been set free from its control over us. We now see from a higher perspective. Remember that!

All the scriptures testify of Christ Jesus giving us revelation of Him. The revelation of Jesus brings us into an intimate union with Him. This union provides our abundance. The Bible is not a book of rules and regulations to follow. The religious system will throw us back on the hamster wheel of performance under the law.

Remember, the law (Old Covenant) brings with it the illusion of imperfection. It creates distance from God and a delay of all He has already accomplished for us. Jesus set us free from the law by fulfilling the law. (Matthew 5:17-20)

Love brought us into a relationship with God through common union (communion). Dear ones: He is drawing near to you. Your heart burns with the desire to know Him. He reveals Himself to you.

John 5:39-40

> *"You search and keep on searching and examining the Scriptures because you think that in them you have eternal life, and yet it is those [very Scriptures] that testify about Me; and still you are unwilling to come to Me so that you may have life."*

Once, I was reading the Word when the pages disappeared for an instant, and I found myself gazing at Him. He was smiling at me. The testimonies of Him drew me with such a desire to know Him and see Him intimately. It is always about union with Him. Allow yourself to be drawn to Him -you will be rewarded, I promise!

Being Doers of the Word of God...

I love Francis DuToits' expression about us being God's poem: James 1:22-25 (Mirror)

> *"Give the mirror-word your undivided attention; do not underestimate yourself. Make the calculation There can only be one logical conclusion: your authentic origin is mirrored in the word. You are God's poem; let his voice make poetry of your life. (We are His workmanship; created in Christ Jesus for good works. Eph. 2:10) For if anyone only listens to the word [a]without obeying it, he is like a man who looks very carefully at his natural face in a mirror; or once he has looked at himself and gone away, he immediately forgets [a]what he looked like. But he who looks carefully into the perfect law, the law of liberty, and faithfully abides by it, not having become a [careless] listener who forgets but [a]an active doer [who obeys], he will be blessed and favored by God in what he does [in his life of obedience]."*

Looking, listening, and doing. It seems so natural, right? The goal is to internalize the Word by identifying personally with what God says and does. We seek to imitate Him as a child imitates his parent. He wants us to live out of our authentic life in the spirit and reap those benefits as His beloved child.

I decided this was my number one priority; to know Him and imitate Him. We can only do this when we give Him our undivided attention. When we do this, we see our authentic origin in the word. We listen, and we do. Obeying the Word is not a legalistic mandate. To obey the Word is to love the Word and what He has already done for us through Jesus. It is undoubtedly a yielding to His love. Numerous times, I may not have understood or felt like "obeying" the Word, but I have never been disappointed when I did. He never fails to amaze me. We always come out on top when we follow His lead. His Truth always brings freedom.

Remember looking into the Word of liberty (Bible) is looking at Jesus, the One who liberated us into our authentic identity. This is the best advice that the Lord gave to me: "Don't look at yourself according to the flesh (natural man). Look at yourself by My Spirit." Friends, this frees us to inhabit our birthright in Christ!

II Cor 3:17

> " Now the Lord is the Spirit, and where the Spirit of the Lord is, there is liberty [emancipation from bondage, true freedom]."

It is by His spirit that we are free. Not by anything we could attain ourselves. No performing or forcing can provide this kind of freedom.

Chapter 15
The Mind of Christ...

I Cor 2:16

> *"For who has known or understood the mind (the counsels and purposes) of the Lord so as to guide and instruct Him and give Him knowledge? But we have the mind of Christ (the Messiah) and do hold the thoughts (feelings and purposes) of His heart."*

I can't tell you the many times I have felt pretty much insane! I could not control the mind traffic that was speeding through my head. My thought life was a dumping ground for every horrific thought imaginable. These thoughts always brought feelings of guilt and condemnation. I was miserable. Then I learned and saw in the Word of God that we have been given the Mind of Christ. Also, we have the authority to take these thoughts captive! This is good news for us. Our minds are no longer a dumping ground for the enemy of our soul to torment us!

II Cor 10:4-6

> *"For the weapons of our warfare are not physical [weapons of flesh and blood], but they are mighty before God for the overthrow and destruction of strongholds. Inasmuch as we] refute arguments and theories and reasonings and every proud and lofty thing that sets itself up against the [true] knowledge of God; and we lead every thought and purpose away captive into the obedience of Christ (the Messiah, the Anointed One), Being in readiness to punish every [insubor-*

dinate for his] disobedience, when your own submission and obedience [as a church] are fully secured and complete."

OK, let's take this from the top!

I was more than ready to overthrow and destroy what mindsets were trying to destroy me, but I didn't know how! I knew I was helpless in and of myself; I tried. But God said His weapons of warfare are of the spirit, the supernatural, and are all-powerful. He said that these weapons would cause every thought to be imprisoned and rendered powerless. Now, we are talking in my language! He has given us the ability to disengage perceptions that have held us captive in the deep fortresses in our heads! God only knows how much I needed freedom from this torment! Let me at it!

EVERYTHING that has the audacity to exalt and position itself against God; every idea, conversation, and argument against the knowledge of God, is cast down and exposed. It can be a mere invention of our imagination because the enemy's lies will bring dark perversion and destroy anyone and anything. We are not to be a dumping ground for lies and deception. Everything that attacks our redeemed identity and innocence will be exposed and stands in the crosshairs of our supernatural weapons. The light of the revelation of what Jesus Christ accomplished and who we genuinely are - blows the lie into oblivion.

Doesn't that just ignite the faith within you?! Here's your strategy for obliterating the lies: *Listen* (to who God says you are); *Aim* (the supernatural weapon of Truth), and *Fire* (The Word of God) by speaking the truth. Simple.

Let us yield our ears to the One which genuinely resonates in our spirits. Do not be tempted by the darts of the enemy: stinging criticism, accusations, condemnation, and guilt are his weapons of warfare.

Let us rise up! Know these Truths: Jesus has restored and given us back authority and dominion. He has already freed us. We have been given inside information - The Mind of Christ. (This is the original Hard Drive containing the most incredible Mind of the Creator of the universe, God).

Let's choose to be like-minded with Him!! All we have to do is decide not to trade the truth for the lie!

Come into your right mind. His mind is in you! We are to echo the mind of Christ; He is the mastermind personified within us! It makes logical and perfect sense that we are one with Him. His thoughts, feelings, and purposes are within us.

We are not striving to become. Holy Spirit empowers us to be who we already are by faith. We are not trying to be someone better than we were before. That's a performance-based mentality. We are to celebrate who we are in Him. This "being" is the revelation. As a result, we are changed and act accordingly, in line with our true selves. We are like God, made in His image from the very beginning.

The Word calls this being SOBER-minded, thinking like Jesus.

I Pet 5:8

> *"Be well balanced (temperate, sober of mind), be vigilant and cautious at all times; for that enemy of yours, the devil, roams around like a lion roaring [[a]in fierce hunger], seeking someone to seize upon and devour."*

I was easy prey. I did not know who I was. I believed all the lies and I was a prisoner in my mind. I was reduced to an inferior being and came under the influence and dominion of deception. I became a servant to the enemy. NOT ANY-MORE – Thank the Lord!! I now remind the enemy that he is a defeated foe and powerless. Decide to stop empowering a disempowered devil!

The Lord says to you, Come into your rightful place, my son and daughter. You are forgiven, yes, even in this current situation. Let me lead you out into victory. I love you!

Being Double Minded...

Are we sound or double-minded?

James 1:8

> *"Being a double-minded man, unstable and restless in all his ways [in It is unsound to reason against the truth. It is not soundness of the mind of Christ to contradict the truth. Natural reasoning, and thinking, will cause us to be unstable, insecure, doubting, fearful. everything he thinks, feels, or decides]."*

As I have shared – I was double-minded, in fact, schizo-phrenic. I lived two contrary ways of thinking and doing. I am delighted to share that I am now sound-minded because I have learned to acknowledge the Mind of Christ within me. I am now free to experience the wholeness of Truth, organic to our being. What a relief to experience being confident in what I am thinking and doing.

If you would like this "sound mind," I recommend get-ting acquainted with what God says in His word. Get fa-miliar with His language and instruction. This will stop the double-mindedness and set you free. You will be alert and identify the lies and temptations contrary to the Truth. The following verse is especially illuminating:

James 1:2 (Mirror)

> *"Temptations and contradictions come in different shapes, sizes and intervals; their intention is always to suck you into their energy field. However, my friends, your joy in who you know you are leads you out triumphantly every time."*

Let's not get sucked in! Jesus bore temptation on the cross for us (Isaiah 53; I Cor.10:13). We can say NO to the lure. We are in authority. It's a wonderful feeling to turn my head from temptation, whatever that may look like. It could be the temptation of sickness, fear, torment, and the like. When sin comes knocking at your door, say no! Look to the One who bore it all. We have the victory in the victorious One. Reminder, we don't fight for victory; we fight FROM victory. We speak the Word of God from this victorious position. We fight (which has been won) in the sense of standing in the finished work of Jesus. Jesus said, "It is finished", and… "It is written" (Matthew 4:1-11)

We are empowered by His inner strength to live the overcoming life.

Phil 4:13

> *"I can do all things [which He has called me to do] through Him who strengthens and empowers me [to fulfill His purpose—I am*
>
> *self-sufficient in Christ's sufficiency; I am ready for anything and equal to anything through Him who infuses me with inner strength and confident peace.]"*

Chapter 16
Believing God...

I have had trust issues since I can remember. I have had a life up until now filled with broken dreams, betrayal, and meanness, and as a result, I became hopeless. You have heard the saying, "Insanity is doing the same thing over and over again and expecting different results."
Well, that was me on the treadmill of insanity. I became acutely aware that nothing I was doing was working. Even that thought was a miracle. I had nothing to lose. I was finally encouraged to trust God in all areas of my life. My mentors added that "He is the only trustworthy One."

It was almost impossible to tell a person like me to stop manipulating God and people to get my needs met. To suggest confiding in God was a significant challenge. (As if He didn't know everything) I had a history of trusting in people and things that betrayed and disappointed me. I couldn't even trust myself. I was encouraged to just believe and receive what Jesus did for me. I was hoping, in my heart, that the things He said were true. I had questions. Lots of them. He was so patient and kind to me during this process.

This was one question I had for the Lord, "How do I trust you?"

His Answer, "Faith. I have given you the grace to trust."

I'm not even sure I understood that answer, but I had to find out. This is what I learned. Grace is the divine influence upon our hearts and is the reflection of Him in our lives. Grace enables us; it is His divine empowerment.

Trust is to have confidence or to have faith in. When we trust Him; we are confident and can confide in Him.

These two things, grace and trust give us an inward certainty that allows us to change our mind by what He says.

Heb 3:6

> *"But Christ is faithful as a Son over His [Father's] house. And we are His house if we hold fast our confidence and sense of triumph in our hope [in Christ].*

Eph.1:13

> *"The Holy Spirit gives guarantee to the fact of your faith, like the stamp of a signet ring that certifies a document. You are in Him!"*

God says to hold fast to our hope (confidence). We spoke about this word earlier. To hope is to expect and anticipate with pleasure. As I immersed myself in the Word of God, confidence/trust in Him began to rise in my spirit. I began to see He is unlike anyone.

Rom 5:5 (Mirror)

> *"This kind of hope does not disappoint; the gift of the Holy Spirit completes our every expectation and ignites the love of God within us like an artesian well."*

I like the way Elizabeth Enlow defines it: "HOPE IS THE ABILITY TO EXPECT GOD TO BE GOOD TO YOU." This definition is true! Allow His hope to be imparted to you!

God is good. He is love, and He is worthy of our trust. He will never disappoint us nor set us up for failure. You can count on Him. Let me share the most endearing couple of examples of this love in my life:

I met my wonderful husband, Joseph, three years after I moved into the house I bought. We got married, and we decided to stay in that home. 10 Years later, Joseph took off for heaven, and I became a widow. God was with me in a profound loving way in my deepest need. He soothed my emotions and answered important questions I had for Him about his passing. He graced me with revelation and understanding. He gave me visions of Joseph in heaven. He allowed me to see Joseph enter heaven, and my Dad greeted him. This vision immensely comforted my soul. God went beyond what I could think, dream, or imagine to give me peace. This experience would require another book to unpack, but needless to say, this deepened my faith in Him tremendously. My love for Him is unshakeable. Yes, I get challenged, but I quickly recalibrate!

God also helped me financially during this time. Something that should have caused ruin turned out to be a blessing in the long run. When Joseph passed, I found it impossible to pay for the mortgage, and long story short, because of the type of loan I originally had on the home – it allowed me to file for bankruptcy while remaining in the house. In the end, I was able to come out of bankruptcy and restore my good credit! I had to trust God to meet my needs and be my everything. He saw the beginning from the end, and He had my back. By trusting God, I lacked for nothing and lived well. (Side note – currently, I am selling my home to be with my family, but I will have a profit that will allow me to buy another house!). God is trustworthy. He is eager to pour out His goodness on you, His Beloved.

Whatever seems impossible to you, turn to Him in trust and He will make all things attainable. (Matthew 19:26) Why does He make all things possible for us? Because He loves us. There is no greater love. (John 15:13) This is exactly why we have faith in Him. God's goodness is our assurance of our hope that is in our hearts.

Heb 11:1-3

> *"Now faith is the assurance (title deed, confirmation) of things hoped for (divinely guaranteed), and the evidence of things not seen [the conviction of their reality—faith comprehends as fact what cannot be experienced by the physical senses]. For by this [kind of] faith the [a]men of old gained [divine] approval. By faith [that is, with an inherent trust and enduring confidence in the power, wisdom and goodness of God] we understand that the worlds (universe, ages) were framed and created [formed, put in order, and equipped for their intended purpose] by the word of God, so that what is seen was not made out of things which are visible."*

That's a mouthful. Essentially, when we believe in Him (trust Him) we are confidently expecting Him to keep His Word. He divinely guarantees it! With our indwelling faith, we believe in the spiritual reality of the Kingdom of God. It is inherent in us. With God's love for us, we have been given authority over this natural world, and our faith materializes this superior life here on earth.

John 6:29

> *"This is the work of God; your belief (Trust) in the One whom he has sent."*

We did not invent faith; it was God's faith, to begin with. Just believe and see.

God's Word says that we are saved by grace through faith

in Christ Jesus and not by our own effort or works.

Ephesians 2:8 (Mirror)

> *"Your salvation is not a reward for good behavior! It was a grace thing from start to finish; you had no hand in it. Even the gift to believe simply reflects his faith!"*

By grace, you and I are being saved from the 'Not I am' lie. All the lies of who we are not! Grace reveals who we are, and the faith of God persuades us of it.

It is all by His grace. We rest because He has already finished all the work. Grace is our state of being IN HIM. The work we do is to believe Him. Believe, and we shall see the Glory of God - on earth as it is in Heaven!

We have the joy and privilege of participating and seeing people, relationships, circumstances, and all of creation transformed by God's loving will. We exercise our authority and watch the restoration of all things take place by speaking the Word of God. Power is released, and every conflict, every distortion of man's own making, is transfigured by the spoken Word and brought into God's will. We have hope and confidence in Him because we know He is who He says He is and does what He says He will do!

The Word of God formed and created everything we see.

Col 1:16

> *"Everything that is, begins in him; whether in the heavenly realm or upon the earth, visible or invisible, he is the original blueprint of every order of justice and every level of authority, be it kingdoms or governments, principalities or jurisdictions; the original form of all things were founded by him and created for him."*

We make the invisible realm visible by speaking the Word of God. (Heb.11:3) This is how He created and how we restore all things. This is exercising our authority, and dominion as Sons and Daughters of whom Jesus is the head.

He has never broken His Word to me, and He will never break His Word to you. It may turn out differently sometimes than how we think it should go. But it will always be for our best. He is the most incredible loving Father.

His heart is deeply gratified when we trust Him.

Hebrews 11:6

"Without faith it is impossible to please God."

Faith is the foundational basis for our relationships – earthly and heavenly. Without faith – there can be no genuine relationship. Think about a husband and wife's relationship. If either of them lacked faith in the other, what kind of marriage would you have? It is faith that pleases God, not good or bad behavior. (Heb. 10:35) He is pleased because He has the best for us and does not want us to settle for anything less than the best.

My previous relationships without God were all about performance and never about faith. That was my M.O. Good behavior or bad, damned if I did and damned if I didn't. The problem is: I didn't, and I couldn't. All the things I did to work at gaining approval to please man were exhausting. My antics were never good enough and never would be. It is worth repeating: Jesus set us free from the law of performance. It is so much simpler with God. All we have to do is trust Him, and His heart gets blessed! This is a reciprocal blessing, as in all marriages. Giving and receiving faith in each other is a bi-blessing!

We are not His servants. We are His friends. He shares His heart with us. (John 15:15) Faith gives us an understanding of God, and trust develops from our union with Him.

Put another way, trusting in God means believing what he says about Himself, you, and the world. His Word is true and unchangeable. To be clear, trusting is a choice, not a feeling.

While choosing to trust Him, His grace will bring you into the revelation of your freedom from sin and all its consequences – because He said so. This revelation will shape your thoughts.

Rom 12:3

> *"His grace gift inspires me to say to you that your thinking must be consistent with everything that is within you according to the measure of faith that God has apportioned to every individual."*

The only accurate way to understand ourselves is by who God is and by what he does for us, not by what we are and what we do for him. I finally saw it! The light bulb went on in my heart and allow it to go on in yours! He already gave us the faith to believe Him. We do not have to strive to get faith - or work it up. It is His faith, and He has been gifted to us. That is how we got it in the first place. How can we have anything unless He gave it to us first?

Don't buy the lie that you don't have enough faith to believe. We have the faithfulness of God. That is all that is necessary. We can increase our faith by building on what He has given us. We build our faith by hearing the Word of God. Truth is we are In the One who is faith.

Choosing to Speak the Word of God...

Let's meditate and build on our faith in speaking the Word of God. It is life-giving for us. Putting this into practice is another good choice.

Prov 18:21

> *"Death and life are in the power of the tongue, and they who indulge in it shall eat the fruit of it [for death or life]."*

As they say, "This is where the rubber meets the road". As we have learned, the Word of God IS God, and it IS Truth. He created the whole universe with His word. (Heb.11:3). The Word accomplishes what He sends it to do. It will never return void. (Is.55:11)

Jesus said to speak the Word and trust God that He will do what He says!

Mark 11:22-24

> *"And Jesus, replying, said to them, Have faith in God [constantly]. Truly I tell you, whoever says to this mountain, Be lifted up and thrown into the sea! and does not doubt at all in his heart but believes that what he says will take place, it will be done for him. For this reason I am telling you, whatever you ask for in prayer, believe (trust and be confident) that it is granted to you, and you will [get it]."*

The Greek translation, in this text, for 'Have faith in God', is accurately translated: Have the faith OF God. Full, perfect, effectual faith in Him is the kind of faith He has gifted us. God said to speak to mountains. In other words, speak to whatever conflict or distortion exists in this natural realm that does not agree with the Word, the superior life of God. Speak to it with His Word, and the conflict and deformities must conform to the will of God by the Word of God.

We do not ask it to; we declare the Word from the authority and dominion God has given us. That word "ask", in Greek, is "to demand or declare." We are to declare the victory of God in all things. His Word is preeminent. Remember, our fight is FROM victory; not trying to get the victory. We are enforcing what Jesus says.

Jesus put us in position for acquisition. We shall expect to acquire all that He obtained for us. So, we declare and change every aspect of our lives and creation to be in harmony with His will.

Our faith will be explosive once we find out the authority we have been granted. All of the creation gladly responds to the declaration of the Word. They are waiting to come into the liberty that the sons and daughters of God have. (Romans 8:22) Everything is put in subjection to the believer!

Our faith is only because of what He has already accomplished. Remember, we are co-included in His resurrection, ascension, and enthronement. It is His faith that is resident in us. When we speak His Word, it resonates within us! We are the ones that will govern and guide the restoration of all things. We are releasing all creation from bondage. We are expanding the Kingdom of God on earth - as it is in Heaven by declaring the Word of God.

Let's agree to exercise our faith and speak to our mountains and say what He says about ourselves and our circumstances. Expect life-altering effects internally and externally. I do this NOW. I have declared wellness to the animals and brought back to life injured birds and a drowned lizard; I spoke to my cat, and she was healed. Even my plants came back to life! I have declared healing in relationships and freedom to tormented people who were set free. People I declared over were delivered of cancer, and deaf ears opened to hear. It is endless what our loving Lord does when we declare His Word!

Let's speak His Word of life to everything...

He is faithful to His Word and us. He spoke to my heart and said to me, 'I say what I mean, and I mean what I say.'

I started speaking His words of life to myself, my family, my friends, and life situations. I have experienced such freedom and restoration in all areas of my life, and He says the best is yet to come. The best is yet to come for you, my friend.

Rom 10:9 Amp

> *"Because if you acknowledge and confess with your mouth that Jesus is Lord [recognizing His power, authority, and majesty as God], and believe in your heart that God raised Him from the dead, you will be saved."*

The word "saved" means "sozo" in Greek. It denotes the very life of God; every aspect of His life applies to every area of our lives. The Word of God is the very saving transformative creative power of God. The Holy Spirit is the transformer.

And by God, things do change, and so do we.

I am talking about applying our faith by speaking the Word and its life-changing effects on our lives and others.

We applied and exercised our faith when we accepted the Truth that Jesus is Lord. We were born again. All of humankind was in Him when Jesus was crucified, buried, rose, ascended, and crowned. (Eph.2:1-6) We were healed and received all the abundant life of God. When we acknowledge that Jesus is Lord, the eyes of our spirit are opened to see the Kingdom of God and the knowledge of the Truth.

Truth always is, was, and will be. He never changes. These things are real because Jesus has already attained them, and we are in Him. It became true for us because it is already the Truth. When we acknowledge and apply this Truth, it becomes our experience. Truth brings us love.

Gal 5:6

> *"For [if we are] in Christ Jesus, neither circumcision nor uncircumcision counts for anything, but only faith activated and energized and expressed and working through love. Love sets faith in motion."*

It is so easy to believe when you comprehend His love. Let the love of God wash over you and well up in your spirit.

Chapter 17
God Is Love...

As I come to the end of sharing my personal story with you, I am compelled to share from the depths of my spirit how much you are loved by God. I will let God Himself tell you in His Words.

John 3:16 (Mirror)

> *"The entire cosmos is the object of God's affection! And he is not about to abandon his creation – the gift of his Son is for mankind to realize their origin in him who mirrors their authentic birth – begotten not of flesh but of the Father! In this persuasion the life of the ages echoes within the individual and announces that the days of regret and sense of lost-ness are over!"*

I John 3:2 (Mirror)

> *"Beloved, we know that we are children of God to begin with which means that there can be no future surprises; his manifest likeness is already mirrored in us!...*

I John 4:15

> *"For anyone to see and to say that Jesus is the Son of God is to awaken to the awareness that we are continuously, seamlessly joined in oneness."*

We are One in Love.

I John 4:16

> *"And thus we have come to know and believe the love that God has unveiled within us. God is love. Love is who God is; to live in this place of conscious, constant love, is to live immersed in God and to feel perfectly at home in His dwelling."*

I love this quote by Godfrey Birtill: "You are not alone and adrift in the universe; you are at home in the Father's good pleasure" -The Wine is Alive!

I John 4:17

> *"So now, with us awakening to our full inclusion in this love union, everything is perfect! Its completeness in not compromised in contradiction. Our confident conversation echoes this fellowship even in the face of crisis; because as he is, so are we in this world-our lives are mirrored in Him."*

When faced with life's fears, we need only to remind ourselves that God included us in His seamless union of love. Fear cannot coexist with love.

I John 4:18

> *"Fear cannot co-exist in this love realm. The perfect love union that we are talking about expels fear; fear holds on to an expectation of crisis and judgment (which brings separation) and interprets it as due punishment (a form of Karma). It echoes torment and only registers in someone who does not realize the completeness of their love union (with Father, Son, and Spirit and with one another)."*

Beloved of God, do not f.e.a.r. It is f.alse e.vidence a.ppearing r.eal. (FEAR) These contradictions present you with the temptation to 'buy the lie.' Mainly the lie is to convince you out of who you already are and what you possess. Please don't buy it!

John 12:31,32 (Mirror)

"Now is the judgment of this world; this is the moment where the ruler of the world-system is conclusively cast out! When I am lifted up from the earth, I will draw all of mankind and every definition of judgment unto me!"

The enemy is a defeated foe, and He has been conclusively cast out along with his judgments! Jesus drew all judgment, to Himself, on the Cross. We are pre-forgiven, not guilty, and not condemned.

Another great quote by Francis Du Toit:

"The truth about you is not in your ability to remember the detail of your horrid past-the degree of your hardship, abuse, and suffering is not your salvation- The awakening to your authentic value, your redeemed pre-Adamic innocence and your defining identity is mirrored in Jesus the Christ the Savior of the cosmos! Do not embrace a "mirror" that resembles anything less than the authentic you redeemed and unveiled in HIM!"

God has found a face in you that portrays him more beautifully than the best theology! Your features, your touch, the cadence of your voice, the compassion in your gaze, the lines in your smile, the warmth of your person and presence unveils Him!

I John 4:19-20

"We love because He loved us first! (We did not invent this fellowship; we are invited into the fellowship of the Father and the Son!). In that day you will know that we are in seamless union with one another! I am in my Father, you are in me, and I am in you! We are inseparable in love. We awaken to the reality of our redeemed oneness."

We are "in that day" beloved!

I John 1:2

"The same life that was face to face with the Father from the beginning, has now dawned on us! The infinite life of the Father became visible before our eyes in a human person!"

Father God was visible in Jesus, and now, Jesus is visible in us! I will close with this powerful prayer for you...

Ephesians 1:18

"I pray that your thoughts will be flooded with light and inspired insight; that you may know how precious you are to him. What God possesses in your redeemed innocence is his treasure and the glorious trophy of his inheritance! You are God's portion. You are the sum total of his assets and the measure of his wealth!"

Believe!

God's Personal Word to You...

"You have always been, you are, and always will be, perfectly loved by Me."

ABOUT THE AUTHOR

Dr. Linda Busuttil, Associate Pastor, has helped pioneer and facilitates the work of Solid Rock Alive in Cottonwood, AZ.

Linda is a prophetic voice delivering a powerful Kingdom message based on fresh revelation bringing inner healing and freedom to people's hearts. She is mandated to speak God's truth, partnering with the Holy Spirit in power. People experience a life change and the tangible Presence of God's love and joy. She has taught and preached in many venues as a conference speaker.

She believes the greatest delivering power to transform a life comes from the experiential Truth that one possesses the Mind of Christ; discovering who you already are; made in the image and likeness of God. She is dedicated and passionate to set people free from bondage of any kind, into their God-given liberty, and have them embrace their living reality in Christ.

She founded Walking Free Sedona, a City Wide; Walk-A-Thon Fundraising Event to Raise Public Awareness, Liberate, and Restore Those from Modern Day Sex Slavery. She has served as President of the Northern Arizona Coalition Against Human Trafficking.

She is also an entrepreneur, a successful business owner, an Apostolic Pastor, and a leader in the marketplace. Currently, she enjoys co-creating with God in the Real Estate Industry. Linda earned her Doctorate of Ministry from Crown Institute under the Founder and Professor Stan Newton.

Linda is available as a guest speaker for events or groups. She may be contacted at: lindabusuttil@gmail.com

Books may be purchased directly from Amazon, Solid Rock Church in Cottonwood, AZ and Glorybound Publishing.

https://solidrockaliveaz.com/

https://gloryboundpublishing.com/

https://www.amazon.com/

Made in the USA
Columbia, SC
18 August 2023